Chapter Seven

THE GOD CONCLUSION

The Memoirs of

Wg Cdr. R. PIFF C.Eng.RAF(Retd)

Order this book online at www.trafford.com/07-2991
or email orders@trafford.com

Most Trafford titles are also available at major online book retailers.

Note for Librarians: A cataloguing record for this book is available from Library and Archives Canada at www.collectionscanada.ca/amicus/index-e.html

Printed in Victoria, BC, Canada.

ISBN: 978-1-4251-6486-7

We at Trafford believe that it is the responsibility of us all, as both individuals and corporations, to make choices that are environmentally and socially sound. You, in turn, are supporting this responsible conduct each time you purchase a Trafford book, or make use of our publishing services. To find out how you are helping, please visit www.trafford.com/responsiblepublishing.html

Our mission is to efficiently provide the world's finest, most comprehensive book publishing service, enabling every author to experience success. To find out how to publish your book, your way, and have it available worldwide, visit us online at www.trafford.com/10510

www.trafford.com

North America & international
toll-free: 1 888 232 4444 (USA & Canada)
phone: 250 383 6864 ♦ fax: 250 383 6804 ♦ email: info@trafford.com

The United Kingdom & Europe
phone: +44 (0)1865 487 395 ♦ local rate: 0845 230 9601
facsimile: +44 (0)1865 481 507 ♦ email: info.uk@trafford.com

10 9 8 7 6

Preface

The purpose of this book is to put into autobiographical context, the account of my after death experience (ADE) from a prolonged heart stoppage, a pivotal chapter in my 92 year long life, which entailed three months in hospital in 1983.

I refer to it as being 'after death' rather than the usual 'near death experience' (NDE), for I was in effect classified as dead, and treated accordingly.

By recounting my life prior to the occurrence, including 37 years RAF service bridging the 6 years of the war, will let the reader know to whom it happened.

Then to summarize the subsequent 37 years of my retirement in Farnborough, Hants, leading up to the cataphatic consequence of the ADE, in the concluding chapter.

My hoard of memorabilia, journals and jottings, have served as spools from which I drew strands in spinning this tapestry of my life, which may at times seem like a tangled web.

I also apologise for any punctuation and grammatical gaffes, for now nearing 93, with an inoperable aneurysm of the abdominal aorta, there is little time for proper proof procedure prior to printing. I make no excuse for my liberal use of, what has been a life-long love, alliteration.

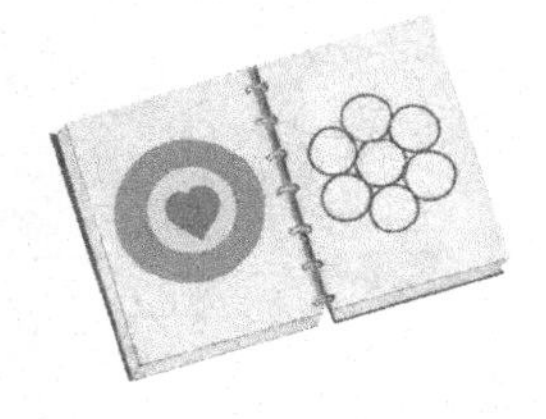

Dedication

I dedicate this book to all who are
committed to care in the community.

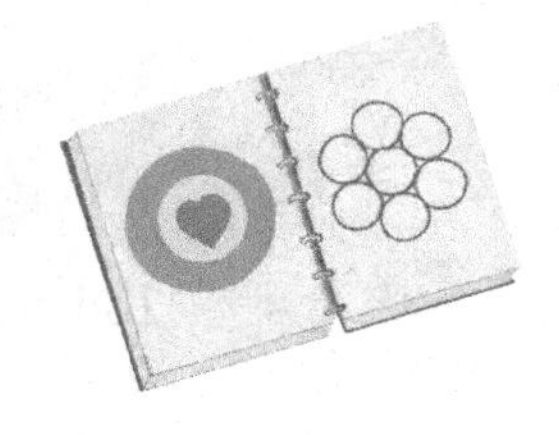

Contents

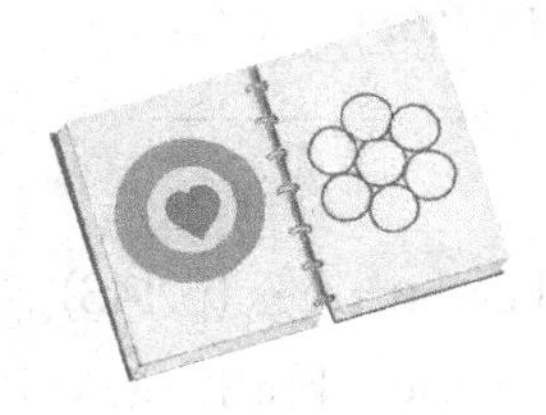

Chapter 1

'Out of This World'

Propped up on a stretcher in an ambulance parked in Boundary Road, Farnborough, I was waiting for my wife Victoria (Vicky) to accompany me to Aldershot for urgent admission to the Cambridge Military Hospital, following a heart attack. It was the afternoon of 3 January 1983, statistically the peak time of the year for this to occur. My G.P. who was waiting with me, had rung the hospital, as my condition was deteriorating.

Through the open doors of the ambulance I could see the house which had been built to our own specification during my second tour of duty here at the Royal Aircraft Establishment, prior to my retirement in 1971, after 37 years service in the Royal Air Force. It stood well back from the road, in an acre of land alongside a block of four maisonettes, which I had previously purchased individually, during and since my former posting to Farnborough in 1955.

In the garden stood the avenue of tall cedar trees (p.143) which had lined the carriageway to Castleden Hall, once a prep-school for Eton, the buttressed walls of the fives court remaining on my land. After the war it was replaced by the R.A.E. Apprentice School which later became the Farnborough College of Technology, adjoining my property, and where Vicky and I were now in charge of the bookshop.

"What can she be doing" said the doctor anxiously, for at that time ambulances were not equipped with paramedic facilities. I visualised her, bewildered by the turn of events and a sleepless night, gathering up what I would need to take to the hospital, and telling her step-daughter Georgina (Gina), who lived next door, of her father's predicament.

"She'll not be long" I murmured. Long enough however, for me to wonder when I would return, in view of the County Council's proposed enlargement of the college. Provisional plans to build around my boundaries would adversely affect our privacy and potential development of the site. It was also clear that a preferable lay-out for the extension would be possible if they were to purchase my properties. The worry over the Christmas period from this sudden turn of events, may well have contributed to my heart attack.

At last I heard the front door close and the sound of hurried footsteps on the long gravel path. She replaced the doctor on the seat beside the stretcher, and as the doors were slammed shut, his parting words to the driver were "as quickly as possible." Rummaging beneath the blanket Vicky re-assuringly took hold of my hand as we sped along Queens Avenue to the hospital. 'Not a promising start to the New Year', were the words written in her diary.

The Cambridge Military Hospital which opened in 1873 is an imposing edifice on high ground overlooking the N.E. Hampshire countryside. At a side entrance I was transferred on to a trolley and an intra-venous tube inserted in the back of my hand. Then I was hurriedly wheeled along the main corridor, some 200 yards, with Vicky breaking into a trot alongside, to Emergency Ward 2A, the intensive care unit. This was a large square room with six widely spaced beds, several already occupied. Curtains were drawn around mine whilst preliminary tests were carried out and monitoring equipment and a drip connected.

Meanwhile my wife was given tea at the ward sister's desk and she came to the bedside when the curtains were pulled back. It was now late afternoon in bleak mid-winter and as 'the shades of night were falling fast' I persuaded her to return home by taxi.

Alone again, my thoughts went back to previous treatment here when I was so favourably impressed with the thoroughness of the investigations and the referral availability to specialist units. Further back, during my first appointment at the R.A.E., I recalled my former wife's admission here, one of her many periods in hospital during a long illness from which she eventually died in 1967. So I was not unfamiliar with the place and its history which goes back to the days of the Duke of Cambridge, once C in C of the Army, who fought in the Crimean War, and after whom the hospital was named. This is all reflected in the long Florence Nightingale type wards, supervised by Queen Alexandra army nursing sisters in their scarlet capes and white starched headdress.

The minutes ticked away on the wall clock, supper trays had been collected and the night-duty staff was arriving. With the atmosphere of quiet efficiency I was feeling a little less apprehensive. Then quite suddenly I somehow felt I was losing a grip on reality, the bed seemed to tilt and I had a compelling urge to escape from it. Simultaneously the alarm bell on the wall beside the large letters AMSET (Army Medical Service Emergency Team) set off by my monitoring equipment, shattered the calm as the team quickly converged towards me, some collecting apparatus on the way. And then I lost consciousness.

Next I experienced being out-of-my-body looking down from above the bed watching the army doctor and nurses repeatedly trying to resuscitate me with defibrillator pads on my chest. I was somehow urging them to keep on trying until I saw the doctor remove the stethoscope from around the neck, look at the clock and noting down the time, before departing through the curtains.

Knowing they had given up, I then had an inside-the body experience trying to massage my static heart muscle, to no effect.

What follows is impossible to adequately describe in words. So ineffable in fact, that I can only attempt to do so by using feeble analogies and 'as if' as a prefix. Having left my body I was aware of being at perfect peace in a dark tunnel-like space with a glow of light at the far end. Its luminosity becoming ever brighter gave an impression 'as if' travelling swiftly towards its source.

Suddenly I came to an abrupt halt. It seemed 'as if' I was at what would be the orchestra pit in a theatre, with darkness behind me and a brightly lit stage in front. There was no perspective or back to the scene which stretched endlessly in all directions and was so appealing that I had to cross-over into the light. Entering an atmosphere of sublime tranquility which further transcends all linguistic description, I was met by what seemed like, a floating mass of amorphous beings, moving to a soft melodic rhythm.

A group of six emerged from the throng, surrounding me in a circle, and though not yet knowing their identity, I was aware that each had been in close contact with me in the past. At intervals, members of the group changed places with others who had also known me. Then suddenly, a messenger-like figure appeared from behind the screen shielding the source of the light, with instructions that I must leave this supernatural realm and return to my body to deal with my earthly problems. Feeling great sorrow at having to leave this empyrean enclave, I left knowing that one day I would return.

As I re-entered my body I found myself laid out on a stretcher on a high bracketed shelf in a cupboard-like compartment. The only light was coming through the half-open door from the corridor outside. As I tried to sit up, the sheet covering me fell from my face, which triggered off a sudden scuffling of feet below me, presumably the orderlies who had carried me in here from the I.C.U.

Once again all went blank until I became a miniature version of myself in R.A.F. uniform, inside a small rubber-like bell-tent from which I was trying to escape. Being unable to find the opening, I repeatedly called out my rank and service number, trying to establish my identity. Then bending down I lifted the skirt of the tent; amazingly this coincided with the doctor raising my eyelid and the rubber tent became the oxygen mask over my face. As I drifted into consciousness, I realised I was back in the I.C.U.

I heard the nurses being told to keep talking to me and one of them held my hand.

From her Geordie accent I later recognised her as one of those who tended me during my long stay in hospital. Like all the other members of the staff she was very reticent about the nights events; seemingly a conspiracy of silence. However before she left to get married, I did learn that the other patients in the I.C.U. were all hurriedly transferred to different wards, before I was moved back in there as its sole occupant.

In the early hours my bed was moved to near the night sister's desk; the ward lights were switched off and I fell asleep. Suddenly I awoke and though still dark, with the light from the desk I could see a figure in an old-fashioned nursing uniform, long grey skirt and cape, sitting at the foot of my bed. I gripped the mattress to make sure I was wide awake. She looked like an old woman but then speaking in a young lady-like voice she said "I have been sitting here watching you and you are going to be alright, so I will leave you now". With that she got up and walked across to the swing doors which she passed through without them opening.

Seeing I was awake, the night sister asked if I was alright and came and plumped-up my pillows. "I'm feeling fine" I said which was rather an understatement, for the apparition of the Grey Lady and her remarks seemed like a significant stepping-stone on the way to recovery, and I went to sleep again.

The arrival of the day staff woke me up and I was the centre of much attention. Several medical officers in their army greatcoats, stopped by on the way to their wards, to peer at me through the glass panelled doors, opening them to take a closer look. The word had obviously got around the various messes at breakfast time, about last nights occurrence.

A further insight as to what had happened was when I discovered sticking plaster on my buttocks, covering a cadaveric cotton wool plug, commensurate with certification of clinical death. I drew the sister's attention to this which she quickly removed, and her being very taciturn in the process. I did not pursue the matter.

I was wondering whether my wife had been informed when she suddenly arrived, as she did every day bless her, whilst managing the college bookshop on her own. She was ushered into the sister's office and notified, to some extent, on my situation.

That afternoon Captain John Quinn the male nurse entered the ward with two civilians. With my eyes closed, but not asleep, I listened to them talking about the new synchronous defibrillator which their firm had loaned to the hospital on trial. Apparently it automatically discharges the high voltage at a precise moment during contraction of the heart muscle, whilst existing equipment tended to be a 'hit or miss' affair. As they approached me, the Captain touched my bed post with his foot and said "without it he wouldn't be here" I heard a cost of £15,000 being mentioned for the equipment, and I felt like sitting-up and signing a cheque on the spot. Now they are widely available in hospitals and ambulances, main railway stations and many public places, costing about two to three thousand pounds.

After a few more days I was transferred from intensive care to Ward No 2.

'For tho' from out our bourne of Time and Place
The flood may bear me far,
I hope to see my Pilot face to face
when I have crossed the bar.'

(Tennyson 'Crossing the Bar')

Now in this long and lofty ward, with its thirty or so beds, is where I would be spending the next three months, until after Easter, the normal routine recovery period in hospital from a heart attack being only one week. The patient in a bed opposite was transferred from the I.C.U. on the night of my attack. From his look of astonishment when he saw me, he had presumably witnessed my body being removed that night, on a stretcher. One afternoon he had a large number of visitors who stared at me with open-mouthed incredulity, whilst he was relating the incident to them. I had intended to chat with him when I was able to get out of bed, but he was discharged within a few days.

I was under the care of Colonel Cormack and his assistant Captain Outhwaite, and the dedicated sisters and nurses under Matron Hennessy. She it was who told me never to shave-off the beard which I had acquired whilst in hospital.

There was some discussion as to whether I should be transferred to the military hospital at Woolwich for an angiogram to investigate any possible damage to the heart muscle and valves. Not yet being well enough to be moved, it was decided to follow the advice of Voltaire and 'let nature take its course'; needless to say, helped by carefully prescribed medication.

My body clock being out-of-phase I kept altering my watch, and on being allowed out of bed, other cognitive faculties had to be re-learnt, such routine matters as which way round to sit on the loo!

Towards the end of January I developed a high temperature and my teeth were chattering. Various tests revealed I had a congestion of the left lung and I was stripped naked and given five hours of electric-fan therapy. This was followed by aspiration of water from the lung, and anti-coagulant injections for a suspected clot. Later I was taken by ambulance, accompanied by two nurses, to St Luke's Hospital in Guildford, for a scan in the nuclear medical department.

In early February I was being visited by Vicky, my sister Cissie, and Gina, when I became short of breath with a rapid pulse rate. I was given oxygen and quickly taken back into the Emergency Ward, leaving my visitors somewhat shaken. After a few days of tests, and an adjustment of medication, I was moved back into Ward 2.

Once whilst talking with a group of nurses round my bed, out of the blue, mention was made of the Grey Lady ghost, reported to have been seen in the hospital over the years, by both patient's and members of staff. This was news to me; neither had I yet mentioned my encounter to anyone. The legend was that during the Great War, whilst nursing her wounded fiancée, she inadvertently administered an overdose of medicine which resulted in his death, and subsequently, her suicide. However, the positive effect of her message 'that I was going to be alright', with of course that from my 'after death' experience; I was now making gradual progress on the way to recovery.

Another step in this direction came from a visit by my late brother's son Christopher and wife Christine. She had suffered a series of facial operations for the removal of malignant tumours involving the loss of one eye, and other parts replaced with bionic implants and prosthesis. Bravely overcoming the tragedy, she set out to help others with facial disfigurement by forming a charity known as 'Let's Face It', and also writing a book bearing the same title, followed by several TV appearances on the subject. Such was her empathy regarding my plight that some sort of cathartic chord must have been struck between us, and I broke down and sobbed my heart out on her shoulder, wetting her long flowing locks. Its beneficial effect was remarkable in the way it cleared my inner turbulence, and I slept soundly that night.

A strictly observed ward routine was a period of silence after the midday meal when curtains were drawn, whilst patients rested. I often took this opportunity to reflect and make notes on my present situation, and to contemplate the alternative decisions I would have to choose, regarding the County Council's 'Sword of Damocles' dangling over my head.

My steroid medication was gradually reduced as I regained stamina. This was helped by physiotherapy sessions practicing diaphragm breathing, which has become a regular routine.

One spring day I was allowed to venture outside the ward to get some fresh air. Providing me with a warm Army combat jacket, the nurses watched as I descended the flight of steps outside the rear of the ward, onto a path at the back of the hospital. It was truly exhilarating to see the magnificent view overlooking budding trees, down to Aldershot town, and daffodils about to bloom, a harbinger of spring and a new life.

A dental examination and Orthopantamagraph revealed that three extractions would be necessary and it was considered better for this to be dealt with whilst still in hospital. The anaesthetists, in discussion with the doctors decided against a general anaesthetic, and that I would be sedated with Valium. Having been prepared and clothed in a white robe, I was wheeled into the main operating theatre. The Valium already taking effect I felt like some emperor, and gave a regal wave to folk passing in the corridor. Sitting up on a raised platform in the theatre, felt like being on a throne looking down on my minions in their overalls and masks, and I happily counted out loud as each painless extraction took place.

On 30th March, my 67th birthday, I was allowed a visit home by taxi. On the way I stopped at a florist and bought an armful of daffodils which I gave to Vicky as she arrived back from her stint at the college bookshop. Fortunately she had already dismantled the Aldershot off-shoot with the help of Barbara and Clive Moulding, two of the college lecturers who have remained close friends ever since. We now also knew of someone interested in taking over the business.

Seeing the backlog of work building up in the garden after my twelve weeks away, and thinking ahead, taking into account my advancing years, it was becoming clearer as to which way our decision was heading concerning plans for the college extension.

Contemplating a few days convalescence accompanied by Vicky, who also needed a break, I suggested a booking at the nearby Frensham Pond Hotel. This was approved and we stayed there midst its pleasant surroundings from 5-9April. Once whilst strolling around the pond, we cleared the air coming to a joint decision to offer up the Boundary Road properties to the County Council.

On 11th April I was discharged to outpatients for a monthly appointment with Colonel Cormack. It was on one of these visits the following year he informed me of his retirement, and that on future visits I would be seeing his replacement. I thanked him profusely for all he had done for me, and shook hands. Just as I was leaving he said "before you go, I must tell you that you nearly made the Guinness Book of Records, the length of time your heart stopped."

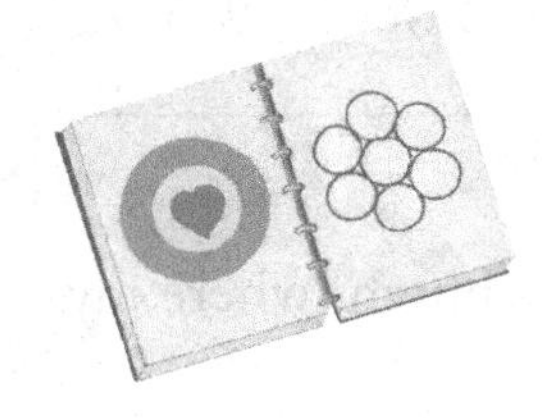

Chapter 2

'Thursdays Child Has Far to Go'

i Early Days

I was born during the Great War on 30 March 1916 in the 'Hospital for Women' in London's Euston Road, arguably within the sound of Bow Bells. Later the hospital was renamed 'The Elizabeth Garrett Anderson' in memory of the first English lady doctor, when she died in 1917.

My mother Cecilia Helen, had been admitted three weeks early due to complications with binovular conception, when only one of twin foetus survives – the 'vanishing twin syndrome'. Such is the lottery of life, I being the lucky one, and also left-handed as is usually the case.

My mother being a devout Roman Catholic, I was baptised when just three weeks old, at the Holy Trinity Church,

Brook Green, Hammersmith, our parish church, where my brother Charles was an altar server.

A copy of 'The Times' which I have for the day I was born, refers to William Willett's daylight saving scheme to be introduced as British Summertime, on 21 May 1916, hoping it would save three million tons of coal annually. Weather conditions that winter were the worst for forty years. It also mentions that Lloyd George, the Prime Minister, had persuaded King George V to declare that he and the royal household would be teetotal for the duration of the war.

Attention is drawn to the severe rationing of food, and the scandalous selling of song-birds for consumption, by a well-known store in Piccadilly.

By 1917 rations were halved by the stranglehold of German U Boats. Malnutrition may have contributed to my retarded growth in early years. Of this I was teased when an advertisement for Virol, a malt supplement, depicted an emaciated child contrasted with a robust one, before and after its use, me resembling the former figure.

My father (1880-1959) was at this time serving in a balloon section of the Royal Flying Corps on the Western Front. Later he was transferred to the infantry along with many others, to make good the mounting number of casualties suffered at Verdun and the Somme. Whilst serving in the Sherwood Forest regiment he was wounded in the chest and brought back on a stretcher to Liverpool, where my mother went to visit him in May 1918.

One Christmas is when my memory first flashes into focus. I recall being cradled in a crib of straw, swathed in swaddling clothes, as part of a live nativity tableau, at the Sacred Heart convent in Hammersmith Broadway. The nuns having seen me in my high pram when my mother came to meet my sisters Cissie and Eileen from the convent school, must have thought I was suitable for the role. Apparently it was a prevalent practice at the time to have a live child in the manger, a precedent provided by the play 'The Miracle' then revived, with Diana Cooper as the Madonna.

Sulgrave Road where we lived formed a loop off the main road between Shepherds Bush and Hammersmith. Our home No 83 was a 3 storey Victorian terrace house, still bearing marks of that era with brass stair rods, removed weekly for polishing, china knobbed bell-levers at the side of marble fireplaces, and sash windows fitted with wooden slatted Venetian blinds. The welcoming warmth in winter of the burnished kitchen range with brass-topped fireguard, the gas lighting and paraffin lamps, lent a feeling of permanence in the changing world in which I grew up with my brothers and sisters.

My maternal grandmother and her spinster daughter, with a talking African parrot lived only a few doors away at

No 75. With our other nearby relatives frequently visiting, as did family friends, many connected with the church, all added to a feeling of belonging. I remember our house being blessed by Father Sutton, the certificate being framed and proudly displayed.

Opposite was a pathway leading to a row of arches supporting the elevated section of the Metropolitan railway. Each arch housed some form of business undertaking. The first one, a stones throw from our house, was a farrier's forge. I liked watching a horse being re-shod, the red hot iron shoe taken with tongs from the blazing hand-pumped furnace, shaped on the anvil, and then the unforgettable smell of the smoke as it was nailed to the upturned hoof, held between the leather covered legs of Mr Lovell.

Horse drawn vehicles and donkey carts still accounted for a substantial proportion of the traffic, and kerb-side troughs were available. Once I saw a horse ambulance rescuing a horse which had stumbled, the broken wooden shaft having pierced its flank.

Funeral carriages drawn by sable steeds with black plumed bridles were a common sight at a time when folk died more often at home, where they remained until the funeral, neighbours blinds being drawn as a mark of respect.

Each day during the Royal Tournament at the nearby Olympia, a troop of Horse Guards would trot along our road on early morning exercise. Once I also remember seeing from an upstairs window, a flock of sheep being driven along, never knowing for where they were bound.

At the age of three I started school at the convent in the infant class. It wasn't a 'playgroup' or 'nursery school', but the bottom rung of the ladder of suitably graded full-time elementary education, progressing upwards in different classrooms to the age of seven. The boys then left to attend boy's schools, and the girls staying on to the age of fourteen, conforming with the prevailing pattern of single-sex education.

I walked to school with my sisters, a mile each way twice a day, there being no such things as school meals. In the morning we stopped at the dairy, next to the Palais de Danse, where horses for the milk floats were stabled. I was provided with a drink of fresh milk to help combat my retarded growth. It was poured from a churn into a half-pint can with hinged lid, as used for doorstep delivery.

Invariably somewhere along the way would be road repair work in progress, with a watchman in a canvas shelter guarding the pile of tarred wood blocks which formed the footing of the road, under a surface of sprayed hot tar and shingle. Chopped-up, the old blocks being replaced, made effective fire-lighters, readily collected in sacks by local lads. The workmen would be seated on planks in the shelter awaiting their breakfast of sausages and bacon, sizzling on the coke brazier, the smell competing with that of the hot tar.

There would be unemployed wartime soldiers wearing their medals and selling matches. Others known as sandwich board men, trailed along the gutter with advertising placards front and rear, suspended from their shoulders. I now consider professional sportsmen having to display sponsorship names on their shirts, to be equally demeaning.

I can recall being in the classroom abutting the Hammersmith Road, on the first Armistice Remembrance Day, when we all stood up as the traffic outside was halted for the two minute silence at 11am.

I remember Charles taking over his sister's dolls house and converting the main room into a church sanctuary with the altar set for high mass, the clergy being clothes peg dolls, garbed in the appropriate coloured vestments for the season and Feast days of the church year. Ten years older than me, he was now working in the City as an office boy with the financiers Rose, Van Cutsem. Always meticulously dressed, with hard collar and three-piece suit, the trousers being pressed every Saturday morning. When this was done, he would set the ironing board up as an altar and take me through the routine of serving at low mass, with makeshift wine and water cruets. Apart from learning the Latin responses, it was necessary to know on which side of the altar to place the missal and stand, for the different stages of the mass.

At the age of six I was chosen by the nuns to learn by heart a fund-raising sermon which I was to deliver on Parents Day, dressed as a priest in cassock and cotta, and a biretta which I still have, specially made for my then small head. Eileen had the task of coaching me and came the day, we were waiting in the corridor outside the assembly hall, whilst she put me through a final rehearsal. The door was opened and I made my entry led by a nun to the steps of a makeshift pulpit. Seeing all those upturned faces, including my mother's with my baby brother Bernard (b. 22 September 1920) in her arms, was somewhat scary but I began – 'Dear Reverend Mother and dear children in Jesus Christ – I have been asked on this auspicious occasion to say a few words to you, and seeing the tender age of some among you, my words must indeed be few'. In fact it went on for over another two hundred words, including the purpose, which was a collection for the badly needed repair of the convent chapel. It concluded 'May God in his great mercy repay you a hundredfold, my blessing I give you all. In the name of the Father etc', which I performed with my right hand in the approved manner. My mother was proud of me though it was the nearest any of her three sons got to the priesthood, which I am sure would have been her dearest wish.

The chapel referred to was where we assembled for Benediction each Thursday afternoon, joining the girls from the fee-paying secondary school which my sister Eileen attended in due course. Dressed in dark blue alpaca with pale blue collars and white veils, they occupied the pews with padded hassocks, whilst we from the elementary school had to kneel in the aisle on the coarse çoconut matting, the pattern becoming painfully embedded on my bare knees, and in my memory.

There had been a convent and girls school on the site since the reign of Charles II, founded by his catholic consort Queen Catherine of Braganza. It was vacated during the Popish Plot (1628-80) when catholics were banned from London; the Society of the Sacred Heart took over the premises in 1893.

I recall being one of the boy strewers in the procession in the convent grounds celebrating the feast of Corpus Christi. Dressed in red cassocks and carrying a tray of flower heads, we turned round at intervals of so many paces, to throw petals in the path of the oncoming priest carrying the monstrance under a four-masted canopy.

Each school year we moved along the cloister to another classroom. The place was full of statuary and holy pictures, and I remember a tribute displayed to John Travers Cornwall the boy sailor, who at the Battle of Jutland in HMS Chester, though mortally wounded remained at his post awaiting orders, with the dead and wounded lying all around him, and for which he was awarded the Victoria Cross.

Now in my final class at the infant school we were being well grounded in the 4 R's, the fourth, or should I say the first, being 'religion'. This mainly involved learning, parrot fashion, the penny catechism in its question and answer format, covering the Apostles' Creed and the Ten Commandments. Also engraved on our young minds, was the respective punishments for dying with unforgiven mortal or venial sins – eternal life in hell or purgatory. Missing mass on Sunday was a mortal sin. Without believing what we were taught, we were told we had as much chance of going to heaven, as counting the number of grains of sand on the seashore.

As has been attributed to a Jesuit 'give me children to teach to the age of seven, I care not who has them afterwards, they are mine for life'. We shall see. Now having reached that age it was time for me to leave the convent and start at St Mary's boys school in Brook Green.

ii St Marys Demonstration School

My new school was at the top end of Brook Green, an oasis of grass in a peaceful residential district between Hammersmith Broadway and Kensington. It was directly opposite our parish church with its Pugin/Gothic style buttressed walls and bell tower, with a church hall and almshouses.

Catholic foundations had mushroomed in the neighbourhood since the Repeal Act of 1791 to the extent that this neck of the woods became known as Popes Corner.

There were other schools nearby, St Pauls High School for Girls where Gustav Holst the music master wrote most of the *Planet Suites*, and St Pauls boys school with its prep school Colet Court. A boarding house for the latter being in Brook Green, the boys could be seen walking to and from school in their long trouser suits, with Eton collars and top hats.

St Marys School was founded in 1851 as a 'demonstration' school which enabled the students at the adjoining Catholic Teachers College to practice their skills. Their carefully prepared lessons were always welcome and continued after the college was moved in 1925, to the former home of Horace Walpole at Strawberry Hill, Twickenham. The vacated premises were eventually taken over as an extension to Cadby Hall, the Headquarters of Joe Lyons, the large food and catering concern. In the meantime we used the site for cricket and organised games.

Now being allowed out on my own, I was able to walk to school and run errands to local shops for my mother. I remember going to Glandford's a hardware store in the Goldhawk Road, then known as the ironmongers, for a tup-penny block of salt and paraffin, where suspended above the counter was a bunch of chastisement canes for 2d (1p) each, for the correction of children. They were not as foreboding though as the yard long canes in each classroom, along with the strict enforcement of discipline.

On the way to school, passing the synagogue in Brook Green, I always crossed over to the other side of the road, a habit I got from my mother when walking to church, ignoring the common roots of Christianity and Judaism in the Old Testament, which was rarely referred to in school.

The sudden change to an all-male environment, and known only by our surnames, contrasted with my previous predominantly 'petticoat' protected upbringing. The only female I remember entering the school was the L.C.C. nurse, known by the boys as 'Nitty Norah' who combed through our hair with a fine-toothed metal comb dipped in disinfectant, looking for lice.

I soon came to appreciate the need for the discipline to prevent disruption during lessons, and bullying and misbehaviour outside the classroom, some student's coming from the less salubrious streets of Shepherds Bush. I was only caned once, for speaking out of turn, the reason for reprimands always being clearly stated.

Mr Ralph Smith was the much respected headmaster who had held the post since 1902. Tall and upright, in a smart three piece tweed suit with a flower in the lapel, such was his authority and influence on the school, it was usually referred to as Mr Smith's school. It has been said that the nearest thing to a magic wand in education, is a good head teacher – we were certainly under his spell. He gave singing lessons, using a tuning fork and metronome, for which several classes assembled. The repertoire was a medley of traditional ballads and sea shanties, the words being displayed on large sheets hung on the blackboard. With his own wind-up gramophone he endeavoured to further our appreciation of classical music, giving facts about the composers. We all strived to match the rendition of 'Oh for the Wings of a Dove' a popular recording at the time by the boy soprano Ernest Lough.

I was one of those chosen to join the church choir a change, until my voice broke, from being an altar server in the Guild of St Stephen, under my brother Charles, then the

Master of Ceremonies, for which in due course he received Papal recognition from Rome.

Starting with the morning roll-call, in the playground we were assembled by classes into ranks, military fashion, and inspected for clean hands and general turnout. We then filed into the school form by form in an orderly fashion, removing our school caps at the entrance.

There were about thirty boys in each class in straight rows of desks, the inkwells being topped up each morning by the monitor. Much of it found its way onto our fingers as we practised joined up italic writing with nibbed pens. Being left-handed I changed hands when the teacher was looking, so finished up with ink on both hands.

In addition to prayers at the start and finish of each morning and afternoon sessions, there was a daily dose of doctrine. During the first year a priest from across the road would attend to test our readiness for first confession and Holy Communion.

About this time I was experiencing bouts of tonsilitis for which treatment at the time was painting them with swabs of iodine. Their removal along with the adenoids was also much in favour, and sometimes carried out at home on the kitchen table. I avoided this possibility when I ran out of the examination room at the West London hospital, as the doctor with a light strapped to his forehead, was about to look down my throat.

As the state of my health was causing concern, I once fainted in church, it was decided that, like little Paul in 'Dombey and Son', I needed some sea air. A neighbour knew the Reverend Mother of a convent in Littlehampton which ran a boy's home, and arrangements were made for me to spend the summer months there. Taken by my mother, the kindly reception in the convent contrasted with my admittance to the home which turned out to be an orphanage for boys of all ages.

I was allotted a bed in a vast dormitory alongside the cubicle occupied by a nun when on night duty. The first night I sobbed myself to sleep and awoke with the nun at my bedside. Dressed in a long white gown with a night cap replacing the veil and wimple over a shaven head, she had come to change my sheets as I had wet the bed. I later found that I had been spared the thrashing with a birch meted out to the other boys for this offence. Once, I even saw a two year-old being given token admonishment with a sprig, during pottie training.

One morning I went with a nun to meet the boys attending a local school, and on our way down the busy high street, the town clock struck twelve noon. The nun pulled me down to kneel beside her on the gritty pavement whilst she recited the Angelus, parting the stream of pedestrians passing by. With today's motley attire of the religious orders, the nun would not have risked laddering her nylons.

One Saturday morning I remember peering into a room where a dozen or so of the older boys were gathered. Trouser less, they were walking slowly round in a circle, raising their shirts each time they passed in front of a nun who beat their buttocks with a birch. I thought at first that it must be a collective punishment for some group misbehaviour, until I found this ritual being repeated on other Saturday mornings. I was somewhat puzzled at the time as to why the boys involved were invariably giggling.

My mother came to visit me and took me down to the beach. It must have been clear to her how discontented I was, for shortly afterwards I was relieved to be back in the bosom of my family, and my mothers cooking. Trying to unburden myself of my more harrowing experiences I was told I must be imagining things, and was forbidden to mention it again. Being 'bottled-up' is possibly why they remain so memorable to me.

The special mass for first communicants had been held in my absence so I made my First Communion, being allowed first place in the queue to the altar rail, at mass on Sunday 23 October 1923. This I know from the framed commemoration of the event, which hung on the wall at home during my boyhood.

Back at school there was some catching-up required having missed several weeks of the autumn term. Mr Bohen the form master coached me on the arithmetic lessons I had missed, including averages and plotting the curve of compound interest. He also taught us basic science, and without a laboratory, it was remarkable the experiments he managed to demonstrate. On a Bunsen burner, he melted the end of a piece of glass capillary tube which he blew into a small bulb. When cool, this was filled with coloured liquid, and the other end of the tube sealed. He had intended to show the relative reaction of different fillings to changes in temperature but had run out of the glass tubes. I remembered seeing some on a waste dump alongside the Osram electric lamp factory at the bottom of Brook Green. I collected suitable pieces of tube in my satchel to take to Mr Bohen the following day. I was rewarded by being allowed to keep one of the finished thermometers.

Much importance was given to notable dates as the backbone of our history lessons. For this Mr Smith had produced a wall chart, on permanent display, stretching from the skirting to ceiling showing important events from 1066, including monarchical succession.

English lessons once included a homework task to write a short biography of a famous author. Being greatly moved by the death-bed account of little Paul in 'Dombey and Son', I chose Charles Dickens. This entailed visits to the Hammersmith library where you entered on tip-toe through the revolving door and were warned to speak in a hushed whisper. I made copious notes about Dickens' wretched childhood and self tuition. Recounting the successive births of his ten children born to his wife Catherine Hogarth before they parted, left little space to deal with his literary output in the time allotted for us to read aloud our finished effort, in front of the class.

Weekly swimming lessons involved a long walk in double file to the Lime Grove public baths. Apart from the heated pool, smelling strongly of chlorine, there were individual cubicles available to the large proportion of the community without bathrooms. Being situated opposite the Gaumont British Film Studios, later the B.B.C. and near to home, I often saw the coming and going of stars of the silent screen.

A practical class I looked forward to was the art of book-binding under Mr Dean's instruction. When proficient we were allowed to bring a book from home in need of rebinding, on which to practice. Charles' much used copy of 'Liber Usualis' his vade mecum for the Roman Rites and Gregorian plain chant, was ideal for this purpose. After stripping it down and re-stitching the leaves on a taping frame, bolting it together in a press and then hammering the spine brushed with glue heated on the Bunsen burner, it was ready for mounting the hard cover. I had to charge my brother half-a-crown for the gold leaf titling on the spine. He signed and dated the new flyleaf 20 March 1926, just prior to my tenth birthday.

The following May he volunteered as a special constable to help maintain law and order during the General Strike. I remember him returning home late one night from the East End visibly shaken as he removed the police arm-band in silence. School had been suspended and the dastardly deeds I witnessed when allowed out of the house, made me realize what he was up against. At an impressionable age, to see a bus driver and conductor dragged from their vehicle and badly beaten, whilst the bus was set on fire, was hard to forget. So also was the sight of a mob of strikers taunting a mounted policeman in Hammersmith market, pulling him from the saddle, then prodding the frightened horse until it slipped on the cobbled road, landing with its legs in the air. After ten days of this the trade union members apart from the miners, returned to work and normality was gradually restored.

My health having improved, along with my school reports, I was selected to transfer to the Brompton Oratory Central

School in South Kensington, together with several other boys whose families frequented the church. These included Godfrey Pippet, Vicky Barnes and Terry Jones whose father was a pillar of the church and a prominent figure in the parish. His weekly visit to the school in connection with the 'Penny Bank' he had set-up, for which a paying-in book was issued to enter what few coppers we managed to save, included an uplifting talk on the subject of thrift. By starting to build up capital from the most modest means, he explained the exponential effect of compound interest, which in time would create a nest-egg enabling us to help others. He set a good example in this respect with his work for the poor as a leader of the local branch of the Society of St Vincent de Paul.

The many activities connected with the church, choir practice, the 21st Hammersmith Scout Group, which I joined as a wolf cub, and the social functions held in the church hall, ensured that Brook Green remained the hub around which my life revolved, long after leaving St Mary's.

('- and Hammersmith was Heaven beneath the moon of other days'
– Kipling)

iii The Brompton Oratory Boys School

I started at the Brompton Oratory School in Stewarts Grove, South Kensington, at the rear of the Fulham Hospital, in the spring of 1927. The school badge, worn on cap and blazer, represented a tassled Cardinal's hat over the letter O, denoting the Oratorian order of non-diocesan priests constituted by St Philip Neri in Rome in 1575, and introduced into this country by Cardinal Newman in 1848.

Many books have been written about the remarkable life of John Henry Newman (1801-1890), visionary, theologian, poet, mathematician and educationalist, who had entered Oxford University before he was sixteen, and elected Fellow of Oriel College at the age of twenty one. Ordained into the Church of England, he wrote a series of Tracts published in *The Times*, No. 90 stating that the 39 Articles of the Anglican faith were compatible with Roman Catholicism, starting what became known as the Oxford Group, now represented by Anglo Catholicism.

He became an R.C. convert in 1845, joining the Oratorian priesthood in Rome, and later founded the first Catholic public school in this country now located at Woodstock. The Brompton Oratory School which my brother Charles had also attended ten years previously, was classified as a 'Central' school, entry being by selection from Catholic elementary schools. The term central was appropriate in that Newman advocated the 'Via Media' principle, not so much a concessionary compromise, as a 'third way'. I have often since found this to be the best solution to many of life's problems. The importance Newman attached to education was his belief that ignorance lay at the root of all evil and prejudice. His principle that provision should be made for the varying potential of individual pupils, was reflected in the diversity of our curriculum.

The school had a well equipped science laboratory, art studio and handicraft workshop. I always remember the dictum of the woodwork master 'to measure twice and cut once' – useful when making decisions in other situations. The syllabus included secretarial subjects such as Pitman's Shorthand, typing and bookkeeping.

The environment seemed to be more relaxed than at my previous school presumably being selected for our keenness to learn, discipline was self imposed, any serious transgressions being dealt with by the headmaster, Mr Duffy, in his study.

Religious lessons were given by the Oratory Fathers from the Byzantine style church in Knightsbridge. They were less catechismal than at St Mary's, dealing with theology and Newman's writings on moral philosophy. My attendance at church services being so frequent, I once automatically genuflected in the aisle before taking my seat at the Kensington cinema.

Our French teacher, Mr Watkins, played outside left as an amateur for Queens Park Rangers F.C. and when I could afford it, I paid the sixpence entrance fee to watch him play at Loftus Road.

I travelled to school by No 49 bus on the open-top deck, making use of the canvas flap attached to the back of the seats, when it was raining. Many were the times I broke the journey to wander through Kensington Gardens from the Albert Memorial, shuffling through the fallen leaves in the autumn collecting conkers, and across to Victoria Gate on to Bayswater Road. Here were the wicker-basket wheel chairs with attendants, lined up for hire by the elderly to be wheeled through the park, covered with a blanket.

With spring in the air I sometimes started out early for school, crossing the park in reverse. I was reminded of this when some fifty years later I found the poem I wrote at the time, among my late mother's effects. Full of poetic licence and with jibes from my brothers, my urge to enter the realm of 'rhyme and rhythm' went unfulfilled, though it still lingers on. It started with the following verses:

Come step off the highway
At Bayswater Road,
And enter God's garden
Where nature hath strode.

Leave the road far behind you
And make for the pond,
O'er nature's green carpet
Her colour so fond.

But be sure and come early
Hear nature awaken,
Ere the dew off the grass,
The Sun it has taken

See the wandering sheep
All chewing the cud,
And the cheeky red squirrels,
The succulent bud.

It doesn't get much better but goes on to describe on the way home, my venturing into Hyde Park, aptly described as the 'Lungs of London'. Across to the Serpentine, by Peter Pan's statue, along Rotten Row with cantering horses, before it was encroached by the widening of Park Lane, and on to

Speakers Corner at Marble Arch, a focal point in the capital of a far-flung Empire. It all seemed so vibrant and less drab than today, with overseas representatives and their families in native costumes, the swaggering off-duty guardsmen in scarlet tunics, and the droves of nursemaids wheeling bassinets and coachbuilt perambulators, the ayahs in saris. The Norland nannies in starched aprons, brown capes and felt hats, clergy and nuns in religious regalia, the Sisters of Mercy in blue habits and white butterfly headdress, all lent a splash of colour to the scene.

The colourful racing tipster 'Prince Monolulu' in his feathered headdress and multi-coloured satin jacket embroidered with his catchphrase 'I gotta horse' which he bellowed out in a deep husky voice, competing with the raucous ranting of the soap-box orators.

The assortment of attire of the masses grouped around them, bore the evidence of the then more stratified society, when dress indicated class and calling, before the levelling down and casualness in sartorial standards, and the advent of our so-called 'classless society'.

One of the speakers I recall was an ex-prisoner displaying the weals from a recent flogging, whilst advocating the abolition of corporal punishment, which remained in force for certain crimes until the Criminal Justice Act of 1948.

On one occasion I was shocked by an anti-Papist refuting transubstantiation, who took a host from a breast pocket, spat upon it and trod it into the ground. Horrified as I was at the time, it has since reminded me of my own diffidence over the dogmatic interpretation of Christ's commandment at the Last Supper, and that what clung to the roof of my mouth on receiving Holy Communion as a child, was none other than a symbolic commemoration. This remains a stumbling block with many contemplating conversion to Catholicism, and the unification of the church in this country.

Less vociferous was the proselytizing of the late Rev. Lord Soper the Methodist minister who had started his 70 years of soap-box sermons.

Alongside was a fanatic inveighing against the perpetration of archaic architectural features in new buildings, pointing across to the Cumberland Hotel with its embellishment of Corinthian columns, as an example of his disapproval. He was promoting a functional cubic style – a portent of the monstrosities which now blight the landscape.

All of which prompted me to end my poem as follows:

At the end of Hyde Park
Where Marble Arch stands,
Are speakers and hecklers
Grouped together in bands.

If you listen to them
Full of man's discontent,
Your time in God's garden
Will be sadly misspent.

However it was not all doom and gloom, for there was plenty of light relief in the cockney humour and the banter and badinage of the bystanders. Sometimes also, the strains of music drifting across from the bandstand, the like of which have now fallen silent, made it an enjoyable and enlightening experience.

Then it was across to the bus-stop opposite Tyburn convent, where once stood the gallows where Oliver Cromwell was publicly beheaded. There was much for my young mind to ponder over on the way back through Notting Hill on to Shepherds Bush, and the peace of home.

In 1928 the house was wired to be connected to the 110 volt D.C. mains cable being laid in a trench in the road, to replace the gas lighting, the street lamps being similarly converted. There were no electrical appliances at the time, the loud-speaker wireless using a H.T. battery and an accumulator.

It was the era of the big dance bands and I liked listening to the early evening broadcast of Henry Hall or Jack Payne and their orchestras. The wind-up gramophone was much in use, my favourite record being Gershwin's 'Rhapsody in Blue' released in 1926, and to which I still swoon.

Throughout my boyhood I was fascinated with kite flying, making increasingly larger models and stitching the fabric on my mothers treadle sewing machine. Whilst flying a six-foot span version with my younger brother on Wormwood Scrubs, we sent coloured cardboard discs spinning up the tethered line to reach the kite. Two warders came out of the prison to make sure we were not sending coded messages to someone inside.

With the school being conveniently near the South Kensington museums, I spent the lunch-time break visiting whichever the subject for homework dictated. They were ivory towers of learning then, peaceful and quiet, before becoming a type of 'theme park' crowded with tourists. The Imperial War Museum, then in Exhibition Road, with its free cinema showing films about the Great War, was a convenient place to eat my sardine sandwiches. Sometimes I wandered through the terracotta portals of the Natural History Museum with its awe-inspiring cathedral-like interior. The colossal skeleton of a dinosaur and other extinct specimens were exhibited depicting the evolutionary process, which was difficult for me to reconcile with the biblical version of creation.

The aeronautical gallery in the Science Museum was my favourite attraction where the history of flying was portrayed with exhibits from Cody's man-lifting kite to a Supermarine Seaplane of Schneider Trophy fame. My aviation scrapbook was rapidly filling up with cuttings of the pioneering and record breaking flights of the period, such as Lindbergh's solo flight across the Atlantic in 1927. It was of some seminal significance when I painted on the cover, the pale blue RAF flag with its red, white and blue roundel, subconsciously setting the seal on my future vocation.

In my second year at the Oratory I sat for two scholarships, one for entry to a grammar school, the other for a 'trade' school, which today would be labelled with the equally non-academic term 'occupational'. It was a major cross-road in my life when, having passed both exams, I had to decide between the two options. The long list of so-called 'trade' schools, covering diverse specializations, tempted me to follow-up my drawing ability in either engineering or architecture.

Relatives of my father, who were employed in engineering in the Midlands, came to stay with us each year for the Motor car and cycle exhibition at Olympia. After one exhibition they presented my younger brother with a display item from their stand, one of the first juvenile cycles which were later marketed as 'Fairy Cycles'. Listening to their talk of the rapid expansion in engineering, I took their advice, for deep down I knew I wanted a career connected with flying.

Having thus decided, I was selected after two interviews, one with my parents, to join the initial intake of a Junior Technical School as the opening section of the newly built North Western Polytechnic, in Kentish Town, NW6, the three year course commencing after Easter 1929.

My present school, now the London Oratory, having moved to larger premises, is described in the Good Schools Guide as an 'oasis of culture' and is oversubscribed by 4 to 1. Most students go on to university, a substantial number gaining entry to Oxford and Cambridge. It is not surprising that the former PM Mr Blair and his wife sent their sons here, and incidentally a daughter to the Sacred Heart Convent.

The school motto 'Respice Finem' (Look Towards the End) is a pertinent reminder to me now to press ahead with these memoirs and to reach their outcome in the concluding chapter.

iv ***North Western Polytechnic***

The North Western Polytechnic in the Prince of Wales Road, Kentish Town had just been built when, joining the initial entry of the Junior Technical School, we became its first occupants. Its spacious interior included a large theatre type assembly hall with stage and gallery, a gymnasium with communal bath, laboratories, workshops and drawing office all newly equipped and, until other courses commenced later in the year, we had it all to ourselves.

Coming from different schools across London, we were strangers to each other at the first assembly. Greeted by the principal Dr F. E. Rowett, we were given an inaugural address by the headmaster Mr A. E. Jeffery, the inspiring theme of which was the foreword in the first issue of the school magazine, of which I still have a copy. In it he referred to the many problems likely to attend the opening of a new institution and how we would set the example for successive entries to follow. To be worthy of this task we must pursue truth, honesty, sportsmanship and the spirit of give and take, playing the game under all circumstances no matter what sacrifice of self it entails. All of this in the spirit of the school motto: 'To follow the Best'.

Although we benefited from this atmosphere and blazed the trail for future entries, it did not last indefinitely. In 1971 it merged with the Northern Polytechnic noted for its internal strife and disruption. Occupation of the N.W. Polytechnic was the start of radical agitation for student participation in college government and an attempt to turn it into a revolutionary political base.

Now in the same assembly hall where we were being inducted, some fifty years later, screaming students taunted, insulted and spat at Norman Tebbitt, Conservative MP, as he tried to address a meeting there.

Being in the younger age bracket, I started in the middle form. However, at the end of the first term examination I was overall first in class, with an embarrassingly favourable report where the word 'excellent' was used by five different teachers, and I was moved to the top form.

In preparation for the official opening by the Prince of Wales in October 1929, a choir was chosen from those boys whose voices had not yet broken, me included, for the occasion. A singing teacher nominated by the Master of the Kings Music, Sir Edward Elgar, brought us up to concert pitch. On the day, the choir being up in the gallery alongside the band of the Welsh Guards, we had a birds-eye view of the assembly hall filled to capacity, the stage being occupied by the teaching staff in caps and gowns, the board of governors and local dignitaries, awaiting the royal presence. After a delay of half an hour we heard the cheering of the crowds outside as H.R.H. was accompanied to the centre of the stage by the principal and the Mayor of St Pancras, the assembly rising as the band played the National Anthem.

In a rather hesitant address the Prince referred to the lack of outside space for outdoor activities and the need for a suitable facility for sport and team games. As if by royal decree, this was rapidly resolved, a sports field at Parliament Hill being made available every Wednesday afternoon, where we travelled by tube with Mr Lovell, the P.T. teacher.

A smoking cabinet made in the workshop was presented to H.R.H. I wondered what became of it after his abdication as King Edward VIII some years later. The ceremony concluded with the choir, accompanied by the band, singing 'I Vow to Thee my Country' from Gustave Holst's *Jupiter Suite*, the verses written by Cecil Spring Rice.

A small monetary award supplemented the scholarship amounting to £3 per term in the first year, rising to £7 in the second and third years. This was to provide ourselves with drawing instruments, slide rule and log tables. I used one of the first year payments to purchase a brand new roadster bicycle for less than the £3.

Sometimes I cycled the eight miles to school through the back streets via Westbourne Park and Maida Vale, which took an hour each way. Returning home one afternoon my front wheel got caught in the tramlines, a cycling hazard in those days, and I was thrown across the road, luckily missing the oncoming traffic. Badly shaken I rested a while on Shepherds Bush Green.

Occasionally I went by bus to Great Portland Street where I caught a toffee coloured No. 536. This was one of the 'pirate' buses operating prior to the formation of the London Omnibus Company in the early 1930's. They were so called for their practice of picking-up and dropping off passengers on request, racing other buses to hi-jack fares waiting at the recognised stops. I enjoyed the thrill of the chase from the open top upper deck.

More often though, I travelled on the underground from Shepherds Bush station on the Central Line, accompanied by my sisters on their way to work as far as Tottenham Court Road, where I changed onto the Northern Line to Kentish Town. Travelling by tube in 1929 was not the trauma it is today, the brightly-lit new carriages seating passengers even in the peak periods, and I frequently finished some homework in transit.

In my spare time I enjoyed the various attractions in the nearby busy Shepherds Bush market. At one of the stalls was Jack Cohen selling groceries with the slogan 'pile 'em high and sell 'em cheap', who eventually expanded his business into the Tesco supermarket chain, becoming knighted in the process. I remember seeing a baby in a pram parked alongside his stall, and have since realised it was his daughter Shirley born 29 November 1930, who became Dame Shirley Porter, once leader of the Westminster Council.

One parent's day, my mother and brother Charles were talking to Mr Jeffery who remarked that I was like a 'little Greek God'. I was teased by this at home especially when my behaviour deserved a more 'down to earth' description.

The school was split into two houses Kelvin and Faraday representing the two aspects of engineering science, mechanical and electrical. The top form syllabus, apart from algebra, trigonometry, co-ordinate geometry and quadratic equations, went on to differential calculus.

As it was not included in the syllabus, Mr Fleming gave after school lessons in French for those taking the matriculation to qualify for entrance to university. In those days only 3 per cent made it, when a degree in art or science was far more prestigious than the various subjects available for today's 50 per cent target for university entrants.

An article of mine in the School Magazine on the 'Achievements of Science' refers to the introduction of 'talkie' films and proposals for the manufacture of television for home use. Also the airspeed record of 336m.p.h. achieved by Flight Lieutenant Waghorn in the Schneider race at R.A.F. Calshot. In 1931 the Labour government refused to pay for the R.A.F. entry for this international trophy and it was subsequently sponsored by the patriot Lady Lucy Houston a former actress. I listened to this event each year on the radio unaware that one day I would be Engineering Wing adjutant at the flying boat base there.

At the end of my three years in March 1932, my mind was made up to join the R.A.F. as soon as possible. This meant applying for an aircraft apprenticeship at R.A.F. Halton and the entrance examination being later in the year, Mr Jeffery said I could attend appropriate classes as I wished, to keep up-to-date. Having purchased previous examination papers from HM Stationery Office, I felt they were well within my capability, so I spent most of that summer on outdoor pursuits to ensure I would meet the medical requirements. I often cycled along the newly built Western Avenue, one of the first dual carriageways (now the A40), to R.A.F Northolt to watch the take off and landings of the Bulldog biplanes of No. 40 Squadron, and the transport aircraft of No 22 Communication Flight, the forerunner of the Queens Flight.

Eventually I sat the entrance examination in a school off Kingsway and was flabbergasted when I found the question paper bore no resemblance to the earlier ones which I had buttoned-up. I did my best but was not surprised when notified that I had not been selected.

Such set backs can act as a spur, as was the pre-war recruiting poster portraying a sergeant pilot in breeches and puttees in a Middle East setting under a bright blue sky, which always caught my eye. I decided to join as a recruit on the bottom rung of the ladder when I was eighteen, and to take it from there. However the strength of the R.A.F. was then only thirty thousand, and in case the door remained closed, Mr Jeffery suggested that I should in the meantime start a civilian career.

He accompanied me to an interview at Smiths Instrument Co at Staples Corner where I was accepted to gain experience in the instrument workshop prior to transfer to the drawing office. After a few months I found the repetitive adjustments of speedometers rather boring and left to take up a similar offer at the Sperry Co which was nearer to home. The necessary experience was to be gained in the machine shop but when they discovered my competence with the micrometer and Vernier gauge and ability to operate a lathe, I found I was being used as a stand-in for skilled craftsmen, on a comparative pittance.

On hearing about high wages earned on the production line at the Brittania Electric Light Co, a Belgian firm, at Park Royal, I made the necessary change and filled in my time there until my eighteenth birthday, when I applied to enlist.

After a written test at the Air Ministry in Gwydyr House, Whitehall and a medical examination I was accepted. My anxiously awaited call-up date came at the beginning of June when with seven others from different parts of the UK, we were escorted by a flight sergeant on the train from Whitehall to West Drayton. Here we were indoctrinated, measured for our uniform, and on 6 June 1934 took the oath to serve for seven years starting as an aircrafthand in the rank of air-craftsman second class. From here we were transported by a solid-tyred R.A.F. lorry to the Training Depot at Uxbridge, where my long R.A.F. career began.

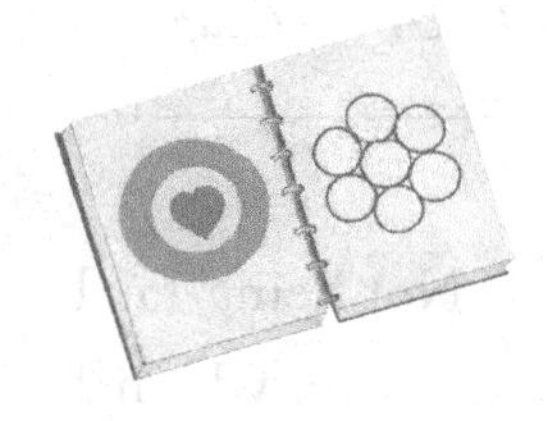

Chapter 3

(1934-1971) 'Rhapsody in Blue' (Per Ardua Ad Astra)

i RAF Pre-War

The RAF Depot at Uxbridge, apart from the two-storey barrack blocks surrounding the parade ground, housed No. 11 Fighter Group HQ, an RAF Hospital, the School of Music home of the Central Band, the various messes and NAAFI canteen, plus a cinema open to the public, at the main gate.

After being kitted out with peaked cap, dog-collar tunic, pantaloons and puttees, there were regular inspections of our turn-out, the polished brass buttons and burnished black boots. Pay was just two shillings a day; one day's pay being deducted for a weekly laundry charge.

Following basic drill and saluting practice, we were allowed out, carrying a black Malacca swagger stick with silver knob embossed with the RAF crest. Not being far I popped home proudly showing-off my new attire, which I also wore for my sister Eileen's wedding on 1 September, brother Charles' twenty-eighth birthday. He had been married two years previously and Cissie one year ago. Brother (Bernard) Benny now nearly fourteen, was at the Salesian College in Battersea.

Later we were issued with the short magazine Lea Enfield rifle and bayonet together with canvas back-pack and harness, haversack and belt. On parade we 'fell-in' in four ranks, the present three line formation was not introduced until 1939. At the morning colour hoisting, when the order was given 'fall out the RC's and Jews' prior to the chaplain's chit-chat, the few concerned had to shoulder arms, take one pace forward or back, depending upon which rank you were in, turn, and march to the edge of the parade ground, order arms and wait for the reverse order.

Fenced off in the transport yard was an obsolete DH9A, forerunner of the Westland Wapiti, on which we were given aircraft handling and prop-swinging instruction. The latter was also done with a Hucks starter, a Model T Ford with overhead shaft which engaged the boss of the propeller.

The Annual Air Display was then held at Hendon and I was among a party of recruits detailed for duty at the 1934 show. I remember the 'crazy instructor/pupil routine' demonstrating recovery from faulty manoeuvres such as falling out of a loop, and hair-raising landing attempts. I later learned that the participants were Fg. Off. Frank Whittle, the inventor of jet propulsion, and one of the Atcherley brothers, known as 'Batchy' who I would one day be a member of his staff, before he retired as Air Marshal.

Classroom work with civilian instructors covered the commitment of RAF units in various overseas locations, and the historical/political purpose of their presence. The vast desert area of Iraq, formerly Mesopotamia, was being successfully policed by five RAF Squadrons and six armoured car units, since Army control was transferred from the War Office in 1922.

It fascinated me to know that Lawrence of Arabia had undergone recruit training here at Uxbridge in 1925 when he joined the RAF as T.E. Shaw, and was still serving in the ranks after I enlisted, before his retirement in 1935 shortly before his fatal motorcycle accident.

In the October I was posted to the Home Aircraft Depot at RAF Henlow in Bedfordshire, with its own railway siding, where major servicing and repair of aircraft was carried out. I was detailed for duty in the Engine Repair Section orderly room, adjoining the office of Wg. Cdr. De Courcey, the section commander. I had my own desk along with two civilian clerks and Sgt. English, the NCO in charge.

Starting work early I was excused morning parade having to prepare the Wg. Cdr's office, light the coke stoves, sort and record the morning mail and deliver it to the various sub-sections, for which I had a service cycle.

I particularly enjoyed visiting the hangars with their variety of aircraft, including the Vickers Vimy, a large biplane which was used for parachuting instruction, the trainee clutching a strut whilst standing on the lower wing on take-off.

Having access to the relevant reference books, it was a good opportunity to learn about RAF management, and technical administration in particular. Some passages in the Pilot's pocket book (not revised until 1937) were diverting such as 'pilots will not wear spurs when flying' – a carry over from when some army officers were transferred to the RAF. Their practice of using ash-plant walking sticks was adopted by RAF officers until abolished by AMO A93 in 1936. In the chapter on Dessert Reconnaissance it states 'in the event of a forced landing, if a dog is carried it should be left tied to the aeroplane'. It details the method of appealing for mercy if attacked by hostile tribesmen, by presentation of the 'Goolie Chit' (a copy of which is in the RAF Museum). The offering of this promissory note was so as to be spared the punishment of castration, or having the genitalia coated with honey and then being tied down over an ant hill, for bombing their villages.

The trooping season was interesting when personnel and families returning by troopship from overseas, were dispersed on disembarkation to units in the UK. I recall a contingent with their kit-bags bearing place names such as Kai Tak, Karachi, Basra, Habaniya, Shallufa and Shaiba. It is not surprising that so many words and phrases from the different languages found their way into RAF vernacular.

Keen though I was to go overseas, I decided it would be wise to firstly qualify in one of the many trades for which training was available. After considering the length and location of different courses, and influenced by Trenchard's dictum 'without armament, there would be no need for an air force', I applied to become an armourer. Seemingly a wise choice, for one day, as the Command Armament Officer at Fighter Command, I would deliver a lecture here at Henlow, to the Officer Cadet Engineering course.

In April 1935 I was posted on a six months armament course at RAF Eastchurch on the Isle of Sheppey. The syllabus covered the range of air armament guns, bombs and pyrotechnics, and associated aiming and installation equipment.

The trainer for bomb aiming practice was a tall tower-like structure where inside at the top, the bomb-aimer, in prone position, adjusted the course-setting bomb sight mounted in front. Below on the floor, was projected a target map moving at a rate representing different aircraft speeds, altitude and drift. After the bomb release button was pressed and an interval equivalent to the time of fall of an actual bomb, the map would stop, the distance of the impact point from the target being measured by the projection of concentric circles to the appropriate scale.

Whilst on leave that summer I cycled to Whitstable, quite a feat with no variable gears. I was spending a few days with Reg Barratt, an old school pal who was staying with local friends of his family. Through them I was introduced to 'Kay' (that being the first letter of her name), who was on holiday and who rather caught my eye. One night a group of us went down to the beach for a moonlight swim. As Kay did not wish to bathe I sat with her against an upturned boat whilst the others splashed about in the sea. We became close companions, and before my departure the following day we exchanged addresses and a peck on the cheek – my very first girlfriend.

On completion of the course I was upgraded to aircraftsman first class and was anxiously awaiting my posting. Meeting Kay I was now doubtful about wanting to go overseas which would mean being away for up to five years. It turned out to be RAF Cranwell in the North of England.

Established in the First World War as a Naval Air Station it was now the RAF Officer Cadet Training College, and also the Electrical and Wireless School. I was attached to the latter, which incidentally started in 1915 in the Old Town Hall at Farnborough.

However, within three months a further posting arrived with a more promising prospect than the lack-lustre landscape of Lincolnshire. It was for a two year tour on the aircraft carrier *H.M.S. Furious* in 801 (FF) Squadron which I joined at its shore base at Eastleigh, in December 1935.

Eastleigh was then a grass airfield with canvas hangars and wooden billets, which has since become Southampton International Airport. 801 a fleet fighter squadron was equipped with the Nimrod single seat aircraft and the Osprey with rear cockpit for the telegraphist/air gunner. The C.O. was Sqn. Ldr. B.V.M. Reynolds who later became Air Marshal and the Governor General of Malta. I was to be responsible for the armament on three of the Nimrods.

Although in the Home Fleet, the *Furious* spent most of the 1930's in the Mediterranean for which we embarked, along with Nos 811 and 822 Squadrons, early in 1936. Starting life as a cruiser in 1917 it was converted into an aircraft carrier without any superstructure above the flight deck, across which arrester wires were raised to catch the hook lowered from the aircraft prior to landing. Lifts fore and aft conveyed aircraft up and down, to and from the hangars below.

There was much to learn about the ships routine and naval regulations, such as stringing and lashing-up the hammock with seven equally spaced lines of rope, in compliance with the wake-up bugle call 'lash-up and stow'. The mess decks being so cramped, several of us slung-up our hammocks at night in the hangers, amid the tethered aircraft.

On our first voyage we encounted heavy seas in the Bay of Biscay, the waves almost reaching the flight deck, and the battened down escort destroyer was so awash, that at times it was out of sight. I soon found my sea legs but was glad when we tied up at Gibraltar alongside *H.M.S. Hood* and *Renown*. Whilst in dock, the inner grass area of the racecourse was used as an airfield.

There were entertaining trips ashore with Flamenco dancers, bull fighting and Tio Pepe at tuppence a glass, in La Linea and Algeciras, before the border was closed during the Spanish Civil war. For this a huge Union Jack was painted on the flight deck to avoid any mistaken attack, as we sailed into the warmth of the Mediterranean for the rest of the winter. We returned to the UK not knowing our next port of call, pending a political decision regarding the Abyssinian crisis.

This was a good opportunity to meet up with Kay, having kept in touch, and to whom I was becoming more and more attached. As a keepsake I used pieces of her letters tightly compressed between different metal washers, on the threaded end of a broken piece of biplane bracing wire, shaped to form the decorative handle of a pointed paper knife. I realised from her letters and our meetings when on shore leave, that she was something of a bluestocking, and that I would have to advance my career before even contemplating the possibility of a future proposal. With this in mind I decided to prepare myself for selection for the keenly contested pilots training course.

After re-provisioning the ship we again set sail, this time for the Eastern end of the Mediterranean. Here we disembarked, all wearing tropical kit with Wolseley helmets, and based in the desert under canvas, south of Alexandria. Much improvisation was needed, aircraft being refuelled from a succession of two gallon cans poured through a chamois leather filter. A Nimrod having force-landed, I went with the recovery team in a Rolls Royce armoured car, travelling many miles across the sand by compass.

Early in 1937 we re-joined the ship bound for Malta where we dropped anchor in Grand Harbour, Valetta. The sun glistening on the water, the golden glow on the limestone battlements, the church bells tolling, and having been there several times since, the scene stays clear in my mind. Shore leave by liberty boat to the quayside where a horse-drawn carriage (gharri) took you into town. Here there was entertainment for all tastes, the Strada Stretta, known as the 'Gut', being the lair of the lascivious 'ladies in waiting'. A group of us visited a bar where a female Austrian string orchestra was performing. Being fascinated by the music and the graceful figure of the harpist with a blonde Teutonic top-knot hairstyle, I stayed for a while after the others left to go elsewhere. Making my way to a table nearer the stage, she gave me a pleasant smile.

Our last evening ashore being a Sunday, there was no live entertainment other than a church dance advertised on the ship's noticeboard. There not being much else, a few of us decided to take a look, arriving during the interval. Met by the priest, we were shown to a table alongside the dance floor, and ordered drinks. Looking across the hall, to my amazement I spotted the 'heavenly harpist' seated at a table. On the spur of the moment I went across to say how much I enjoyed her performance and that unfortunately we would be leaving tomorrow. Smiling gratefully she pointed to a chair for me to sit down. She spoke in broken English and introduced me to a lady with her who I took to be her chaperone, but conversation was interrupted by the band starting again and couples getting up to dance. Raising her eyebrows and nodding towards the floor, we stood up and joined them. Fortunately for me it was a waltz, and being in uniform with an Austrian partner, I felt I only needed a sword and cape to be like some hero in a Strauss operetta.

Seeing her back to the table, she stopped and facing me said 'take me home' and left saying 'I'll see you in the entrance'. Flabbergasted, and knowing I had no money, I went back to my colleagues and asked Cpl. Hayley-Morris for a loan. I told him my plan would be to take a gharri and drop her off, and then carry on back to the ship, and he lent me £2. I made my way to the entrance where she was chatting to the priest and I assumed she was among the many Austrians who, under Italian influence were RC's. It was reminiscent of the church dances I went to at home, under the scrutinous eyes of the parish priest. We left with his blessing and climbed into a waiting gharri.

It was a steep uphill trot, past the Floriana gardens till we reached the apartment block where she was staying. I got out to help her down and bid farewell, but by the time she took my hand she had paid the driver who drove away, as she led me into the building. Her suite on the upper floor had a large bed-sitting room with balcony overlooking the harbour. I noticed various music academy awards along with the Stabat Mater Dolorosa picture of the Virgin Mary, identical to the one we had at home. A rosary with crucifix on the dressing table, along with the angelic symbolism of the practice harp in the corner, all led to a 'pious' atmosphere about the place.

Sitting together on the balcony it was a relief to see the ship in the distance in the moonlight beneath a starry sky. After a while she took the tray of drinks back into the room and re-appeared having let her hair down and disrobed into a silken dressing gown. I took this to mean that it was time for me to leave, but as we went back into the room she took the harp and sat down to play. Placing it between her knees, and with the arpeggio chords plucking at my heart strings, I was in another world as I got up to go, when she had finished playing. She came across, kissed me which I thought meant goodbye. Instead she undid the top button of my tunic saying 'I will see you get back to the ship in time' and departed into the bathroom, leaving the door ajar as she ran a bath.

Did she mean me to join her or merely put my feet up on the couch? My mind was in a turmoil as I sat on the bed wondering what I should do. The pillows looked so inviting in contrast to my hammock, that I was tempted to start unwinding my puttees. Suddenly, I didn't know whether it was the thought of Kay or the consequence of missing the boat, I got up and left, closing the door quietly behind me whilst she was splashing in the bath. I fled down the stairs like Joseph escaping from the bedroom of Potiphar's wife, and strode down the hill. Having plenty of time now I sat in the gardens to collect my thoughts, and dozed off.

Dawn was breaking as I continued on my way. A gharri pulled-up alongside me with two Royal Marines returning to the ship, who offered me a lift. As we reached the dockside the liberty boat was waiting, and with the last of the stragglers aboard, the coxswain cast-off. Approaching the ship we could hear the anchor team being piped to the cable locker and by the time we were aboard the fo'csle, the deafening noise of the anchor chain being wound around the capstan with the accompanying haze of rust, I quickly went amidships down to the mess deck. Passing the ships noticeboard I caught sight of the permanently displayed message of the Oxford Movement, the moral re-armament group – 'Somewhere a woman, mother, sweetheart, wife, waits patiently for your return – spoil not her faith in you by sin or shame'.

Having given Hayley back his £2, shaved and changed into working dress and had breakfast, I hurried to the hangar as the squadrons were piped 'to flying stations', whilst sailing out of the harbour homeward bound.

Now upgraded to Leading Aircraftsman, the squadron commander accepted my application for pilot training and I was interviewed by Capt. Dowding R.N. who gave his approval. I thought how much a pilots wings would enhance my prospects with Kay, a letter with her photo awaiting me at Gibraltar.

Back in the UK I was notified of the interview at the Air Ministry and an appointment for examination at the Central Medical Board, whilst the ship was in dock at Invergordon, and I travelled to London by night train. Though all seemed to go well, I was kept in suspense for several months before knowing the outcome.

In the meantime there was a move afoot for the Fleet Air Arm to be transferred to the Admiralty and I declined the offer to join the Navy. I followed another of Trenchard's dictums that 'the air is indivisible' a subject I will return to later, and just before Christmas 1937 I was posted to No. 17 Squadron at RAF Kenley.

Pleasantly situated in Surrey, only a short train trip to Victoria, it was convenient for meeting Kay who lived in Battersea. Our rendezvous was at Moyses-Stevens the fabulous florist outside the station where she would choose a nosegay from the exotic display. Then after some refreshment, we would visit a cinema, usually the Metropole, where we held hands. When for some reason she could not turn up, I would stroll across Albert Bridge 'just to be on the street where she lived', such was my infatuation.

No 17. Squadron was equipped with Gloster Gauntlets and No. 3 Squadron, also there, had Gladiators. Knowing I was awaiting pilot training the CO gave me some dual flying experience in a Miles Magister, including aerobatics.

The squadron was detached for air firing practice at Sutton Bridge in Norfolk, and then at Filton near Bristol. It was whilst in the huge hangar there, which later housed the Brabazon, that I received the anxiously awaited letter. It was from the De Haviland School of Flying at White Waltham to say that I would be on the course starting in June 1938.

I told Kay the good news and explained that I would be tied-up for a few weeks during the *ab initio* stage of training. Somehow I felt she had been somewhat distant of late but, if anything, this spurred me on to do well, wear the coveted wings, and woo the woman I loved.

Of the twenty two students assembled for elementary flying training, only two of us were RAF airmen and accommodated in separate board and lodging houses. The remainder were potential direct entry pilot officers, subject to completion of the course, and were all together in communal mess quarters. However, we all wore civilian clothes and were on an equal footing during the day.

The instructors were all ex RAF officers under Sq. Ldr. R.W. Reeve DFC, AFC, MM (Ret'd). After ground familiarisation with the Tiger Moth biplane and starting-up its 120 HP engine, we were issued with flying overalls, helmet and goggles, and assigned to a particular instructor for dual flying training. This covered taxying and take-off, medium turns, stalling, gliding and landing for about ten hours before being ready for that first solo. I took a little longer as my first instructor was not very communicative. On making a mistake he would take-over the controls without explaining the situation. There was little de-briefing on landing compared with the others who had a lengthy conflab with their instructors once out of the cockpit. Also, being socially isolated, apart from the occasional meeting in the local, there was little chance for discussion with the other students.

There was a certain amount of classroom work especially when bad weather prevented flying, and I was called upon to impart my knowledge of the various items of armament equipment available.

Having changed instructors I was making good progress and getting the feel of the aircraft, like learning to ride a horse, knowing how to control the beast. After several dual sorties on 22 July, my instructor undid his Sutton harness, climbed out of the cockpit, and slapping the fuselage said 'its all yours, watch out for other aircraft'. It is almost impossible to describe the exhilaration of rising into the sky on your own, for the very first time, with all that power at your fingertips. A once in a lifetime experience which only those who have shared it, will know what I mean. This being followed of course by the apprehension of 'coming back to earth' mentally and literally, and the satisfaction of a classic three-point landing.

I wrote to Kay to tell her the good news, though I was still awaiting a reply to my previous letter. Several successful solo flights followed until one morning I was waiting in the crew room to be summoned for a further sortie, when the mail was distributed. There was one for me which I knew from the hand writing was from Kay, but it was a small white box with silver surround. Obviously a piece of wedding cake and I was flabbergasted when reading on the back, her married surname and new address. Without opening it I stuffed it into my overall pocket just as it was announced that my aircraft was ready, and my mind was in a whirl whilst walking out to the plane.

Strapping myself in I tried to put it out of my mind, taxied and took-off. On the circuit I couldn't believe what was in my pocket and thought of throwing it overboard. Coming into land and not being quite into wind, the starboard wing dropped and just as it was about to touch the ground I opened the throttle, as taught when making a bad approach, to go round again. By the time I levelled the wings, the aircraft had swung round and I was now down-wind and facing aircraft coming in to land. With just sufficient height to clear the perimeter hedge, I climbed to 800 feet and got back on the circuit.

Looking down I could see the fire engine and ambulance getting into position and from the many upturned faces, I could see that I was the cause of some concern. This time I made a perfect three-point landing, feeling that I had made a good recovery from a difficult situation. The outcome was that I would have to undergo a test by the RAF instructor on his next visit from Hendon.

The day he arrived, all student flying had been cancelled due to strong winds, but my test flight went ahead. On each attempt to land, due to the wind, the plane remained airborne, and I knew I had failed. The statement in my log book, boldly written in red ink says 'SUSPENDED FROM FLYING TRAINING AS UNLIKELY TO BECOME AN EFFICIENT SERVICE PILOT' signed W.C. Sheen Flt. Lt. (later Air Vice-Marshal). This following the piece of cake, put the final seal on my dream.

It is rather ironic that the phrase 'piece of cake' was common RAF parlance at the time, meaning something easily accomplished. However, looking back at the course photograph and knowing how few survived the war, I suppose I should be grateful to Kay for that carton of cake.

It was some consolation that I was promoted to Corporal and given the chance to choose my posting. With the growing concern over the possibility of war, I favoured being close to family and friends, and selected RAF Northolt. Gp. Capt. Orlebar of Schneider trophy fame was the station commander and Sqn. Ldr. Gillan was C.O. of No. 111(F) Squadron, which I joined as armament N.C.O. Known as 'downwind Gillan' after his record breaking flight from Edinburgh to London in 48 minutes (408 mph) helped by a northerly wind, which was much publicised. I recall a DH Rapide which he had hired, taking him with colleagues and wives, on a celebratory weekend in France.

No. 111 Squadron was the first to be equipped with Hurricane fighters with its eight fixed Browning guns, but fitted with primitive WW1 ring and bead sighting facility. The firing results at practice camp were far from satisfactory, and we were continually painting spots in different patterns on the hangar doors in order to align the guns to conform to the latest tactical thinking.

A scientist from the Royal Aircraft Establishment at Farnborough, Maurice Hancock, was attached to Northolt to help resolve the problem. In October 1938 he put forward a proposal which led to the design of the gyroscopic gunsight for which he received an award. Development took some while and in the meantime we harmonised the guns on to a single spot at the required range, for a 'head-on' attack. This no doubt contributed to the squadron's success rate at the outbreak of the war.

The ring and bead sight was difficult to see at night and I took a set to the maintenance unit at Kidbrooke to be coated with phosphorescent paint. It was mounted in a box for me to take back whilst the paint was drying, and on the way I called in to see my mother, and jokingly said that the package contained a secret weapon. On reflection, this was not far from the truth, to the extent that the Luftwaffe would have been glad to know that we relied on such elementary equipment, for our front line fighters.

I cashed some savings and bought a one-year-old Austin 10 four door saloon for £60, new cars then costing from £100. My cousin Harold Martin taught me to drive on the then village roads of rural Ruislip nearby, where he lived with his parents, my Aunt Florence and Uncle Harry, and his two sisters, Vera and Joan. The Highway Code at the time described whip signals for horsedrawn traffic, and there were less than one tenth of cars on the road than today, when I passed the driving test which had just been introduced.

Whilst on leave, I drove down to Lyminton where my parents were staying with a maiden aunt. It was about the time of the Munich Crisis, and I became aware of the seriousness of the situation when, late that night I received an immediate recall to duty, by urgent telegram. I rang the orderly officer to say that I would make the return journey first thing in the morning, but I was told to start back at once. My father came with me driving through the night and after dropping him off at home, I was back in Northolt for breakfast.

There was a growing feeling of being on a war footing with the armourers belting-up ammunition around the clock. The station was bursting at the seams with call-up of reservists, the overall manpower of the RAF having more than trebled since I enlisted in 1934. To ease the shortage of accommodation, sleeping-out passes were granted to those with suitable facilities, of which I took advantage. I had the best of both worlds, retaining my room attached to the barrack block of which I was in charge, or alternatively sleeping at home.

These were heady days both at work and play under the gathering war clouds, and a group of us spent much of our hard earned off-duty time in the bright lights of the West End. Parking anywhere, meters not then existing, our evenings began with buying buttonhole carnations from the florist sitting on the steps of the Eros statue in Piccadilly Circus. Then on to our favourite bars in Soho and finishing up at a night club, such as the Blue Lagoon or the Fleur de Leys. At the time I could have written a whole chapter on these soirees, under the title 'Gentlemen Rankers out on the Spree'. My family saloon was exchanged for a Rover sportsmans coupe as being more in keeping with the playboy image of the time.

Brother Charles with his wife Kitty, and small son, were now living in a new house in nearby South Harrow and we kept in touch. My parents had moved to a flat in Brook Green, near the church and our local, the Queenshead. Whilst in the latter one Saturday evening, I met Reg Barratt who was leaving to take his fiancée Madge and her girl friend to a church dance at Our Lady of Victories in High Street, Kensington, and he invited me to join them there.

My introduction to the girl friend, Frances, known as Babs, was a big moment in my life. In a dark green velvet costume, with a far-away look in her eyes, a slightly husky Talulah Bankhead voice, and a matchless dancing partner, I can best describe how I felt in the words of the then popular song from the 1938 Goldwyn Follies 'love walked right in and drove the shadows away'. An ex-Ursuline convent girl, she had just returned from a skiing holiday in Arosa (p.142) with her elder sister Marguerite (Peggy) and Roger Bushell, a barrister and Royal Auxiliary Air Force pilot, with whom Peggy apparently shared a bon vivant lifestyle. Later as a POW he was shot and figured as Big X in the film 'The Great Escape'.

After the last waltz, I drove Babs home and we arranged to meet next morning after High Mass and then on to the Queenshead to meet my brother Charles. During the remaining days of my leave we visited the West End and the then fashionable 'road house' the Thatched Barn, for a dinner/dance.

Promising to keep in touch, I returned to Northolt with my head in the clouds. Now promoted to Sergeant, there was much activity preparing for the possibility of war. The aircraft were dispersed around the perimeter with tented accommodation for aircrew and ground staff.

Sqd. Ldr. Harry Broadhurst (later Air Marshal) was now commanding the squadron and with him we all listened on that fateful Sunday morning 3 September 1939, to the following broadcast by the Prime Minister Neville Chamberlain –

'As no response has been received from the German Chancellor to the ultimatum that all German troops be withdrawn from Poland, a state of war now exists between our two countries'

The CO summoned me to his tent and stressed the importance of a high standard of serviceability of the guns in this situation, for which the squadron motto 'Adstantes' (Standing By) was now appropriate. As if referring to the crossed-swords on the badge above the motto he said 'the guns are now our spearheads, keep them sharp', which meant a low gun stoppage rate. I conveyed his message to the armament tradesmen.

'Now thrive the Armourers'- Shakespeare Henry V Act III

ii *RAF World War II*

Shortly after war was declared I was posted to No. 4 Balloon Centre in Chigwell, Essex, now the Roding Valley nature reserve. This was my tenth move in five years, all to difference parts of the UK, in addition to visiting Gibraltar, Malta and N. Africa during my two years at sea, all of which broadened my outlook on life. As Tony Benn MP once described his RAF experience as being a better education than he had at New College – a better perspective – education is about what happens to you rather than what qualifications you acquire.

Prior to the Battle of Britain in June the following year, the period referred to as the 'Bore War', Balloon Command, situated at the Stanmore HQ of Fighter Command, controlled over a thousand barrage balloons, the biggest concentration centred on London. Capable of being winched to an altitude of five thousand feet, the aim was to deter enemy aircraft from attempting low-level attacks.

I was in charge of the station armoury but was mainly involved with a new device fitted to the balloon cable which it severed when struck by the wing of an aircraft, opening a parachute on the detached cable, disabling the trapped plane. Due to teething trouble a number of balloons were breaking free and 111 Sqn became the champions shooting down eleven of these rogue balloons in one day.

This was my first encounter with the Womens Auxiliary Air Force (WAAF) who formed the larger part of my team, and I found them to be far more diligent and dedicated, than their male counterparts.

During my short time at Chigwell, I was admitted to the Royal Herbert Army hospital at Woolwich with prolonged fever from a peritonsillar abscess. My mother came to see me, taking the opportunity to call on relatives who ran the Director General hostelry nearby. A visit from Babs and her mother Lavinia (Mungar) was a shot in the arm towards my recovery. Now out of bed we had to wear wounded soldiers uniform, a bright blue suit and scarlet tie.

On discharge I made my way across London to spend sick leave at home, where Babs came to tea to meet my parents. She had met my brothers and sisters, as I had her female family, her father Ion Wentworth Hamilton suffering a fatal road accident when she was a child.

Shortly after returning to duty I was posted to No. 1 Air Armament School at RAF Manby in Lincolnshire, on a Senior Armament Instructor's course commencing 2 December 1939.

Viewing this move as an opportunity to advance my career, I completed a postal course of the then widely advertised Pelmanism, so popular and effective that the name found a place in the Oxford Dictionary. Defined as a 'scientific memory training system' its affect on me was that I finished the course, sharing top marks with fellow student Alec Pedder.

This resulted in being retained to instruct future courses, specializing in the theory of bombing, a somewhat esoteric subject involving Pythagorean mathematics, Newton's laws of motion and gravity, navigation, ballistics and the law of probability. Training in its application entailed practice bombing in a variety of aircraft including the Fairey Battle, Blenheim and Wellington, and also the American B17 Flying Fortress and the Hudson.

Babs had moved out of London to 'Westwood' a farmhouse at Nettlebed in Oxfordshire. We got together whenever possible, sometimes meeting halfway in Peterborough. Here we once met my brother Benny then at RAF Upwood with No. 15 Squadron, part of the air striking force in support of the British Expeditionary Force. On 17 June 1940 two of the squadrons' aircraft collided coming out of cloud and one, having a wing ripped off crashed killing all the crew. The other, of which Benny, then aged nineteen, was the navigator, suffered a damaged engine and the pilot ordered him to bale-out, safely landing near Bayeaux, whilst the pilot, Ron Clark was killed attempting to retrieve control of the aircraft.

Later that summer during the 'blitz', I travelled by train via London to Nettlebed, with the engagement ring in my pocket. The train was halted for several hours outside Kings Cross, due to heavy bombing. Eventually on the Underground where the platforms were full of people bedded down for a night's shelter, I managed to get as far as Great Portland Street. On reaching the exit I found the night sky lit-up with incendiary bombs dropping, anti-aircraft guns flashing, and a flaring gas main which had burst nearby, and I quickly retreated. During a lull in the bombing, it now being nearly midnight, I caught a taxi to my sister Cissie's house in Hammersmith. As another raid commenced, I cowered on the floor of the cab on hearing the swish of falling bombs, the driver calmly said 'when you can hear them mate, they're not going to hit you'. How Londoners coped with this for over four months was incredible.

I found Cissie and her two young sons, Michael and Max, down in the cellar, her husband Stan an ARP volunteer prior to joining the army, was involved with a house opposite which was on fire.

Next morning I set off for the calm of Nettlebed, where walking with Babs in the beechwoods, I proposed and we agreed to marry as soon as possible. Her mother (Mungar) took over and arranged the wedding for 11 January 1941 at the Sacred Heart church, Henley-on-Thames, with a reception at the Catherine Wheel, Maidenhead. Her younger sister Rosemary, who was about to join the WAAF, and Sheila her step-sister from Mungar's second marriage to Leonard (Paddy) McDermott, which had ended in divorce, were among the very few guests.

We spent our wedding night at the Catherine Wheel before driving in Babs Morris 8 to Louth, with frequent stops to check the route, as all road signs had been removed, in the possible event of invasion. We stayed at the Masons Arms in Louth until moving into a house in the abandoned holiday resort of Mablethorpe on the NE coast, twelve miles from RAF Manby.

This was a lonely time for Babs for even in what spare time I had I was busy constructing my own idea of a bombsight which would give the pilot a degree of manoeuvrability during run-up to the target, existing bombsights requiring a straight and level approach. I was given the opportunity of testing it out in a Blenheim on two sorties at different heights, with Sqn. Ldr. Simpson as the pilot. The results achieved were sufficiently successful for it to be taken the following day to the Air Ministry by Sqn. Ldr. Richardson for consideration. I heard no more about it since not only was an automatic bombsight under development, but the U.S.

Sperry auto bombsight as used in the B17 Flying Fortress, was shortly made available.

A Sperry flight was formed under Sqn. Ldr. Richardson for training bombing leaders from operational squadrons in its use, and I was to be the instructor, having recently been promoted to Flight Sergeant. With the Sperry bombsight, the automatic pilot is connected to the bombsight, giving the bomb aimer control of the aircraft on approaching the target. With a few days help from a USAF officer and a Sperry representative, we planned a five week course of training using US Hudson aircraft, with which we were now equipped for practice bombing.

I constructed a classroom trainer in the form of a toy battleship target electrically driven across the floor at varying speeds and direction, above which the bombsight was mounted. Unbeknown to me, one of the students had blackened the rubber eyepiece, hoping to give a fellow student a 'black eye'. It so happened we were paid a surprise visit by the Inspector General, Air Marshal Barratt to whom I demonstrated the trainer, positioning him over the bombsight. Although he was unaware of it, I was shocked when he left looking as though he had been in a fight.

We had now moved into a house in Grimoldby on the perimeter of the camp, as Babs was now pregnant, and I was able to get home for lunch. After Christmas she went into

Louth hospital where our son Nicholas Charles was born on 9 January 1942. It was a thrill to visit her and see the lovely baby in her arms. Then a few days later Sqn. Ldr. Richardson called me out of the classroom to tell me the hospital had telephoned to say that my son was seriously ill. He took me to the hospital in his MG sports car, where I found the baby in an oxygen tent in a separate room from Babs, who was very distressed. He was suffering from a respiratory problem which didn't respond to treatment and he died only ten days old.

Mungar came up to help and accompanied me to the funeral where I carried the little white coffin in my arms across a snow-covered cemetery to the grave.

I had previously passed a commissioning selection board at the Air Ministry and was now granted leave pending posting to Uxbridge for the four week officer training course. Up to now, forty bombing leaders had completed the Sperry courses, sadly several did not survive the daylight raids on specific enemy targets; subsequently Bomber Command changed over to mass night raids on German cities. I had flown over two hundred hours with them on bombing practice sorties, in just over six months.

We packed our bags and moved back down South to order my officer's uniform, in preparation for the course commencing at Uxbridge on 11 February 1942.

Peggy arranged to meet us in London the day I collected my uniform, having had the final fitting, at Gieves in Bond Street. She had recently married Joseph the 17th Lord Petre (Joe), then in the Coldstream Guards, in the private chapel at the ancestral home, Ingatestone Hall in Essex. (p.157) The press announcement of the marriage mentioned that they were to have been at the Café de Paris the night it was bombed killing thirty-four including the orchestra, but had cancelled the booking just in time.

Now wearing my new uniform we met her for lunch at the Buttery in the Berkeley Hotel, a popular venue for the pilots of 601 City of London Auxiliary Squadron, some of whom we met, who knew Peggy from her previous engagement to Roger Bushell. After a leisurely lunch, we went shopping in Fortnum & Mason and then to Gunters in Park Lane for tea, unrivalled for its urbane upmarket atmosphere.

Babs stayed with Peggy in a cottage in the grounds at Ingatestone, the Hall being used as a school for the duration of the war, during my month at Uxbridge. Apart from ex-rankers there were direct entry acting pilot officers on the course which meant much foot drill on the old familiar parade ground. NCO aircrew promoted to officer rank, like brother Benny who was commissioned before me, were exempt from this transitional training.

We were billeted in the same old barrack blocks, now better furnished, and the former airmen's cookhouse had been transformed into the more formal setting of an officer's mess. One morning I sat down at a table for breakfast opposite someone reading the morning paper which he politely folded after surreptitiously removing his spectacles. To my astonishment it was my boyhood screen idol, Rex Harrison. After a nod and passing the time of day, having finished his breakfast he got up and left. I wish I had known then that my cousin's daughter Sally Piff and her future husband, a property tycoon, would one day be buying his villa at Cap Ferrat along with his Mediterranean yacht. Somewhat flat-footed on the parade ground, he did not serve for long in the RAF before returning to his thespian pursuits.

The allocation of appointments at the end of the course was anxiously awaited, mine being Station Armament Officer at No. 9 Air Observer School at RAF Penrhos in North Wales. Shortly after arriving I was sent on a brief detachment back to Manby to assist in flight testing a new stabilized automatic bombsight with Mr Maile, a scientist from the Royal Aircraft Establishment at Farnborough. After several sorties in a Hampden at five thousand feet, the results were similar to those achieved with the manually controlled sight line on my own experimental bombsight.

Back at Penrhos, several flights in a Lysander high wing monoplane, had revealed the attractiveness of this part of North Wales, and I started looking for accommodation for Babs to come and join me. However, after only one month I was on the move again, this time to No. 4 Air Gunnery School at Morpeth, where I would be in charge of the instruction staff under Sqn. Ldr. Simpson from Manby. The school was in the process of preparing for training air gunners, for which I had to compile the syllabus and arrange provision of the necessary equipment.

It was a new site in the vicinity of Tramwell Woods, with widely dispersed units, for which I was allocated a motorcycle. We were equipped with the unpopular Blackburn twin-engined Botha with gun turret for air-firing practice. Four test pilots had been killed in them before the problem of its going into an uncontrollable dive, was solved. Unfortunately we also had a fatal accident, and once when flying with a Polish pilot and trainee air gunner, I was alarmed when the airspeed indicator failed, but flying by the 'seat of his pants' we made a safe landing.

There were no married quarters but I discovered a large bungalow in four acres of forestry, which was being vacated. Unfortunately there was no electricity available but I was informed that an overhead supply could be arranged if I provided and erected the necessary pole. Searching the woods

I found a suitable tree already felled which, with the help of colleagues, was stripped and erected just in time for switching-on, prior to Babs arrival.

Commencement of training sessions and meetings was not set on the hour or half-hour but to a precise minute, Sqd. Ldr. Simpson's pet idea to ensure punctuality. Things were going well and I was promoted to Acting Flight Lieutenant as Gunnery Leader, normally an aircrew post.

An entrant on one of the courses was Vicky Barnes a school friend from Brook Green and the Oratory. Slightly older than me and rather dashing I had tended to look up to him, but it was the other way round now when I found him once on fatigue duty, on his hands and knees polishing my office floor. Sadly he was killed on operations in the October, and buried in Hanover war cemetery.

A memorable day was a visit by Marshal of the RAF Viscount Lord Trenchard, 'father of the RAF'. Then aged seventy and wearing uniform, the programme included an address to the assembled school for which I had the privilege of greeting him. Later that day I was in charge of the guard of honour, on his departure.

As Babs was thankfully again expecting, she moved down to London to stay with Cissie in preparation for admittance to Queen Charlottes. Meanwhile I accompanied Sqn. Ldr. Simpson on a five day trip, flying in a Martinet to Chipping

Warden, Little Horwood, Abingdon and Attlebridge near Norwich where Dutch squadrons were based. I remember having a farewell dinner with some of them, all speaking fluent English, in the Castle Hotel, on our final night.

Our daughter Georgina was born on 15 May 1943 (the time of the dam-buster raids), and I travelled down to see her and Babs. I didn't mention that I had been posted to Gibraltar, which thankfully Gp. Capt. Louden the Station Commander, later managed to get cancelled in view of my present circumstances. Alternatively he arranged an interview for me, whilst in London, with Dr Cawood at Thames House, Milbank, for a possible Research and Development project. Awaiting the outcome we returned to Morpeth by night train, with carry-cot, my sisters seeing us off at Kings Cross. Within a short while another overseas posting arrived for which it transpired, I had insufficient grounds for cancellation.

Not knowing the destination, apart from tropical uniform being required, or for how long I would be away from Babs and baby, was very worrying. I moved them with our belongings, in with my parents, now in Lymington, before leaving for embarkation at Liverpool.

We were billeted in private accommodation in Morecombe until the arrival of the troopship *S.S. Dilwara* when we were transported to the dockside, to go aboard with our metal cabin trunks and kit bags. Still not knowing our destination we set sail, and entering the Straits of Gibraltar, I was reminded of my time on *HMS Furious* which had recently made four deliveries of Hurricanes to Malta, followed by a hundred Spitfires later in 1942.

We were held up near Sicily in the aftermath of operation Husky. The island was now in Allied hands having been invaded from North Africa, which had led to a foothold in Southern Italy. The Germans had been misled by bogus papers, stating that the invasion would come from Greece, on a dead body dressed as a naval officer and placed as if washed ashore on an appropriate beach. It was the subject of a post-war BBC programme titled 'The Man who Never Was'.

Whilst here we were transferred to a ship belonging to the British India Steam Navigation Co, there no longer being any doubt about our destination.

Interesting talks were given by the Intelligence Officers regarding events in various theatres of war. Malta, no bigger than the Isle of Wight, had endured twice the tonnage of bombs that fell on London during the worst period of the blitz, for which it was honoured with the title 'The George Cross Island'.

On our way again, through the Suez Canal and the Red Sea, into the Indian Ocean with the heat in these parts, the uniform was now khaki shorts and bush jacket. I often wonder why the latter had not been adopted for wear at home in hot weather and on holiday, with its many pockets, which you miss when having to discard the lined jacket. Certainly a more 'sahib' image than the obnoxious fashion of wearing the shirt outside the trousers 'native' style.

Disembarking at Bombay, the gateway to India, I was temporarily housed with a dozen or so fellow officers, in a large house on the waterfront which only had two lavatories. As most of us had the 'squitters' known as 'Delhi-belly', it was a case of joining the queue clutching ones own packet of Bronco toilet paper.

Just before boarding a train to Delhi for an appointment interview, I was handed a long list of the service personnel in transit and told that I was the officer in charge, without time to ascertain what this might entail. Not being a corridor train it was only possible to make contact with them at the frequent stops, when a supply of fresh water was the main concern. At one station a swarm of monkeys appeared on the carriage roofs, sneaking through open windows to grab anything to eat.

At the interview at RAF HQ New Delhi, my recent background fitted me for posting to No. 7 School of Technical Training being set up at Quetta on the NW frontier, bordering Afghanistan. Having sampled the sights of the city, I set off on another long train journey, in the opposite direction to the theatre of war, to this remote spot some six thousand feet up on a sloping hillside.

On arrival at Quetta, the provincial capital of Baluchistan, a bundle of letters from Babs awaited me, and it was good to know that she had received mine I had sent en route. Writing to let her know about where I was now settled, I asked her to send me some of my civilian clothes, as being far removed from the war zone, mufti was the rule when off duty. Here in the October of 1943, the climate was very pleasant but snow was usual during the winter. Basically the camp was an army depot with Ghurkha and Indian regiments, a staff college, army hospital and public cinema. Apart from the mounted army units, the wide equine involvement in personal transport, polo and hunting, it was not surprising that there was also a popular horse racing track.

My task was to draft a syllabus for updating tradesmen back from the front, on the latest equipment, and arrange such facilities as a twenty five yard firing range, and workshop and classroom resources. Having got the first course started, Flt. Lt. Ken Wadham arrived to take over which meant me losing my acting rank and being demoted to Flying Officer, as his assistant. This gave us both more time for off-duty activities and I joined a riding class run by the Camel Corps, with a turban wearing instructor. The training was thorough, each exercise ending with the order 'recompense your horse'.

White Barracks, where the RAF was located comprised a collection of single-storey staggered buildings constructed since the tragic earthquake of 1935 when every building was destroyed and thirty five thousand killed. Adjacent to the officer's quarters was a stable block which prompted me to take advantage of the offer of an army ex-mount complete with tackle, for a mere one hundred rupees. I settled for Gilpin, a bay gelding, less high spirited than the one previously offered. In addition to my personal bearer, I now employed a sice to look after the horse.

I met Pamela at a mess function and being a keen equestrienne with her own horse, we became riding companions. After introducing Ken to her sister we attended the diverse functions as a foursome, frequenting the officer's club nightly dinner dances with music from a Ghurkha band. Pam's parents were proprietors of the Quetta Hotel where we became family guests and where I stayed for a week after a short spell in hospital. My partnership with Pamela was purely platonic, she, like me, being otherwise attached, her fiancée serving elsewhere as an officer in a Ghurkha unit.

Though usually slow off the mark, Gilpin was a fast sprinter and I entered him for a four furlong handicap race at a Hunt Cup gymkhana meeting on 13 May 1944, the race card which I still have, states my registered colours of blue and primrose stripe. There were thirteen entrants, most with professional jockeys, two starting at scratch. To my amazement we quickly overtook those in front and led all the way to the winning post. The cheers from the airmen, no doubt having backed me at long odds, with the shouts of 'shah-bosh' (well done) were ringing in my ears as I dismounted in the unsaddling enclosure. Pamela drove us back to the mess in her Cadillac, with me clutching the Hunt Cup presented to me with the hundred rupee prize money.

A celebration in the ladies room marked the end of a memorable day but also, as it transpired, the coming to the end of my nine months sojourn in this Shangri-la environment.

Thinking of the hardships being faced by those back home, especially Babs and baby, I felt somewhat guilty. However the armament courses were running to plan with excellent results, as I prepared to move to the Far East war zone at No. 231 Group HQ in Calcutta. Pamela waved me goodbye as I started on my six day train journey via Lahore. We kept in touch for a while and I often wonder how her life progressed, and I still remember her soigné appearance and smiling face.

Calcutta, once the jewel in the crown of the Raj, with its imperial architecture, was reminiscent of England apart from the pavement dwellers and slums, the humid climate and dreaded monsoon season. The headquarters of No. 231 Group, part of the joint USAAF and RAF Strategic Air Force of Eastern Air Command, was in Belvedere House, a former palatial residence of the Governor General, before the capital was transferred to Delhi, in 1922.

Having regained Flight Lieutenant Rank I was assistant to Sqn. Ldr. Basil Charles, the Group Armament Officer for whom I deputised during his prolonged absence in hospital and UK leave. The Liberator bomber squadrons were widely spread on remote airfields at Salbani, Ranchi, Jessore, Dhubalia and Digri, which I frequently visited by air from Alipore. The Japanese advance to the Indian border had been repelled and their task now was the bombing of the transport system and targets in Burma.

Group Captain Leonard Cheshire, still in his mid-twenties, joined the HQ operations staff in September 1944. He had recently been awarded the Victoria Cross for over a hundred operational sorties including low-level target marking and pin-point attacks on V2 launching sites, whilst CO of No. 617 Squadron. He sent for me to advise him of the range of bombing equipment available, and was dismayed at the lack of target illuminating flares. A few days later, I was aboard an Anson at Salbani for the return flight to Alipore. The pilot had started the engines but was waiting for another passenger who was on the tarmac talking to the station commander. It was none other than Gp. Capt. Cheshire who took over from the pilot and the forty five minute flight was the most skilful yet hair-raising, hedge hopping flight imaginable.

His advocacy for low level precision bombing was not proving to be effective when attacking railways, as the bombs were ricocheting off the track. This was overcome by screwing a steel spike in the nose fuse socket of the bomb. I became involved in the manufacture of these two feet spears at various workshops, including backstreet garages. After collecting each day's production, first checking the accuracy of the unfamiliar American thread, I transported them in a Jeep to Alipore for urgent delivery to the squadrons.

For a short while I was detailed as a 'round the clock' escort to Wg. Cdr. John Hallett, demoted to Flt. Lt. whilst in custody awaiting court martial. He had been in charge of RAF Intelligence at General Slim's 14th Army HQ during the preparation period to re-conquer Burma. He was charged with receiving £187,000 in cash from a Prince of Nepal in advance of ten million pounds, for recovered estates from which the owners had fled. This was on the strength of a document bearing the forged signatures of the Supreme Commander Lord Louis Mountbatten and Air Marshal Sir John Baldwin.

I could see from the address of St James' Club, Piccadilly on his trunk, which had previously concealed the cash, and his silk sheets and lavish accoutrements, that he was a London socialite. I was not aware at the time that he knew my sister-in-law Peggy whose husband Lord Petre was also a member of St James' Club. He refused to name his accomplices and was sentenced to fifteen years imprisonment, reduced to ten years, of which he served only six, being released in 1950.

A welcome break was a spell of leave when I experienced the interesting single track train journey up the southern slopes of the Himalayas to Darjeeling at 7,000 feet. It was a popular resort with the US and British service personnel of both sexes, a variety of pastimes being available including pony trekking, ice-skating and dances every evening. It was so bitterly cold after dusk that getting to sleep was difficult but the magnificent sight at dawn of the sun rising from behind the Kanchenjunga Mountain, was some compensation.

Cissie's husband Stan was now an officer in the Scots Fusilier's attached to the 9th Rajput Regt. here in Calcutta. We attended many mess functions together, also travelling by rickshaw to various clubs such as the '300' and the 'Porto Rica'. Another popular venue was Firpos restaurant opposite the Maidan, an open space from where Hurricanes had recently operated, repelling Japanese attacks on the city, the pilots waiting in the restaurant on 'standby'.

Whilst in No. 9 RAF Hospital, recovering from a bout of fever, Stan came to visit me with the sad news that my brother Charles' wife Kitty had died, shortly after giving birth to twin daughters.

Each morning the staff officers assembled for briefing on the war front situation and it was now a matter of following the Japanese retreat. At the beginning of 1945 the race began to reach Rangoon before the summer monsoon. The POW's in the large jail there had been abandoned by the enemy, and the inmates had painted large white letters on the roof 'JAPS GONE-EXTRACT DIGIT'.

The Air Officer Commanding, Air Cdr. 'Tog' Mellersh, summoned me to his office to discuss how best to use the Liberator bomb bays for dropping food and medical supplies, urgently needed by the prisoners, pending their rescue.

V.E. Day on 8 May passed almost unnoticed in the Far East, though we did arrange a brief celebration in the mess, when I fired some signal rockets on the flat roof.

I was again in hospital when some of the POW's arrived for admission. The skeleton like figure carried to the bed next to mine was being filmed by the press. There was obviously a shortage of beds so I got dressed and discharged myself on 23 May.

My name was drawn out of the hat for one months UK leave. The journey started on 9 June by train to Bombay and

Poona to await air transport. This was a short range Dakota with bench type seating and the twenty passengers included several sick personnel being repatriated on medical grounds. There were seven overnight refuelling stops before arrival in the UK at RAF Merryfield (Taunton) on 25 June. I travelled to Brighton where I was met by Babs, and Gina, now two years old and to whom I was a stranger. A lively child we were soon on good terms though my absence has no doubt affected a full fatherly affiliation.

We were staying with Mungar in her large first floor flat in a Regency property in Sussex Square, Brighton, far enough east of the piers and parts frequented by the day trippers. A tunnel in the private gardens led under the coastal road to the promenade and beach. It was a blissful interlude relaxing in the sunshine with Babs and Georgina, and visiting family and friends.

The Far East war was drawing to a close even before the Americans released the atomic bomb on Hiroshima on 6 August from the B.29 in which Gp. Capt. Cheshire VC was an observer. In fact my UK leave stretched to 15 August, V.J. Day, the day WWII ended. Unfortunately this was the day before Babs' twenty-fifth birthday, when she came to see me off from the transit camp at Regents Park. I travelled to Liverpool by special train, and that evening embarked on the half empty troopship 'Strathnaver'. After a leisurely cruise, we arrived in Bombay on 3 September, six years to the day since war was declared.

On my return to Calcutta I found that 231 Group was closing down and I acted as Camp Commandant during the latter stage of its closure. I then became the adjutant at a Rehabilitation Centre where my main task was trying to calm down the unruly conscripts clamouring for priority on the passenger lists to the UK for demobilization. This problem in other places led to fifty thousand RAF personnel going on strike, the biggest single act of defiance in the history of the British forces, and was treated as mutiny.

As a regular, I was expecting to return to the UK early in the New Year when I would have completed two and a half years in India, and the repatriation fever would have subsided. However, to my amazement, I received a posting in the opposite direction to Hong Kong, where brother Benny happened to be stationed at the time. The thought of a further two years away from my loved ones prompted me to apply for my discharge. This was permissible without prejudicing a future application for a permanent commission. My discharge was granted and I was back home for Christmas 1945 on three months release leave, and with a gratuity of four hundred pounds.

iii RAF Post-War

Back home in Brighton, where Eileen and family were now living round the corner on the seafront, and Benny, back from Hong Kong also nearby, we were often together in our local, the Rock Inn. He was awarded the MBE for his wartime service.

With my approaching discharge date and dwindling gratuity, clutching at straws I arranged an interview at the Air Ministry. Much to my relief I was offered a temporary eighteen month's appointment at HQ RAF N. Ireland in Belfast, which I accepted. Starting in March, I found the job included frequent flights from Aldergrove to the various RAF units in N. Ireland and the Outer Hebrides, to supervise the disposal of war-time explosive stocks, prior to closure.

Off-duty I sometimes attended the many horse race meetings and was fascinated by the frenzied fanaticism of the punters, and fluctuating bids of the bookmakers. The latter prevented me from using the 'probability theory' inspired system, which relies on the odds being even. With this, the stake is always the sum of the first and last numbers in the series starting 1-2-3, the first stake therefore being four. Should this win the numbers which formed the stake are crossed out leaving '2' as the next bet. If this wins the series is completed and, having won 6 (4 + 2), you start again. When losing a wager you add it to the series and carry on until all the numbers are deleted, when the balance between winning and losing bets will always be the magic 'plus 6'. Probability should not prolong the series sufficiently to 'break the bank'.

John Maynard Keynes the economist, once hearing that a casino in Ostend was playing roulette without the house number 0, leaving an even chance between black and red, and odd and even numbers, he travelled there overnight and returned with a worthwhile wad of winnings. Over the years such testing of his treatise on probability, may well have accounted for the small fortune he left when he died in 1946.

Making arrangements for Babs and Gina to join me, I booked accommodation in Mrs Blood's guest house opposite the Queens University. The name being boldly displayed on a brass door plate, made me wonder whether she was related to Colonel Blood, the Cromwellian soldier who tried to steal the crown jewels. He was pardoned by King Charles II and given land to settle in Ireland.

In the meantime I received a staff visit from the Command Armament Officer Gp. Capt. L. de V. Chisman CBE, DFC. He had served in Quetta at the time of the earthquake in 1935, and was interested in my more recent tour of duty there. Such was the progress with the disposal of ammunition stocks, he considered I could be spared to fill a vacancy on his staff back at Coastal Command HQ in Northwood.

I broke the news to Babs on her disembarking after an extremely rough crossing. However, the date of our return on 14 June allowed time for sightseeing tours by pony & trap, and a trip across the border to Dublin's fair city.

Coastal Command HQ was in a large country house, the former notorious night-club run by Kate Merrick, which received publicity in the pre-war press pertaining to police corruption. Situated fourteen miles NW of London, I moved in with Cissie and Stan in their large flat in Holland Park, travelling to Brighton at weekends to be with Babs and Gina.

After the terrible winter of deep snow and ice, on 27 April 1947, Babs' younger sister Rosemary married Stefan Michalski, a Polish RAF officer she met during the war when she was in the WAAF. Gina, not quite four was an infant bridesmaid accompanied by her cousin the Hon. John Petre, a year older. I missed the church service at Spanish Place as I was attending the funeral of my mother's elderly cousin Alice Orthey, but was able to join the reception at the Dorchester Hotel. The wedding was reported with photographs in the 'Tatler'.

Searching for somewhere to live with Babs and Gina, I discovered a war damaged property in West Kensington in the final stages of being rebuilt. This conveniently situated corner house, 37 Gunterstone Road, comprised four self-contained flats and two large garages, and the 32 year lease was on offer for £2,200. I borrowed the deposit from my mother, and we moved into the first floor flat in June 1947.

Now 'Air Cdre' Chisman, he was appointed Senior Technical Staff Officer, and he nominated me as his P.A.. Frequent staff visits included the flying-boat base at Calshot, when I took the opportunity to visit my parents now in nearby Lymington. The following March the station armament post there became vacant, for which I successfully applied through the good offices of the Senior Personnel Staff Officer, Wg. Cdr. E.F. Pippet, who was at school with me at the Oratory.

Pending the availability of a married quarter at Calshot, we moved in with my parents, at Lymington. I bought a pre-war Baby Austin 7 to travel the twelve miles to work across Beaulieu Heath, and also to enjoy the beauty of the New Forest area, with Babs and Gina.

Calshot was the base for two Short S.25 Sunderland flying boat squadrons and an Operational Conversion Unit. One of the squadron commanders was a colourful Irish character Sqn. Ldr. David Fitzpatrick, very popular in the mess. He had a notable career during the war and later commanded the Christmas Island base in the Pacific, during the nuclear bomb tests.

It was a pleasantly situated officer's mess, and the anteroom had a sprung dance floor. Years later Calshot changed hands and became an Activities Centre, with the mess now a public house, known as the 'Flying Boat'.

Not being very busy as the station armament officer, I was able to assist the Senior Technical Officer with the task of co-ordinating the work of the specialist sections. During a staff visit by Air Cdre. Chisman I suggested to him the need for a post to be established for this purpose. He told me to submit the proposal in writing detailing the duties involved. This I compiled during the Whitsun off-duty weekend and submitted it to headquarters. Surprisingly, it was quickly accepted and the post of Technical Adjutant was eventually established on all operational stations throughout the RAF. Soon afterwards, having passed the qualifying examination, I was granted a permanent commission.

Now officially in this role I moved into an office in a large hangar at the end of the Spit, overlooking the beach and adjacent to the Tudor castle which now served as a flying control tower. The latter was built in 1540 as part of Henry VIII's chain of coastal defences to counter a possible invasion by the powers of Europe, following his break with the Catholic Church.

In July ten Sunderlands were detached to operate from Lake Finkenwerder near Hamburg, in support of operation Plainfare the joint USAAF/RAF Berlin airlift, transporting supplies to the beleaguered city, in defiance of the Soviet blockade.

Wing Commander Crosbie OC Flying, who led the detachment, temporarily vacated his married quarter which was made available to me and we moved into this large house on the foreshore overlooking the Isle of Wight.

In August, flying in a Sunderland I visited the detachment staying in a former Luftwaffe officers mess still staffed with frauleins. The extent of war-damaged property in Hamburg was beyond belief, still in ruins and roads lined with rubble. Also surprising was the boisterous night life of US and British servicemen in the company of local females.

With the end of the airlift in sight, and then having to vacate the married quarter, prompted me to think of moving on. Considering an overseas posting before Gina was of boarding school age, I thought of Gibraltar as being suitable, from my previous visits and its climate. I made my wishes known to Flt. Lt. Williams, the station adjutant and left the matter in his capable hands. Just before Christmas a posting notice arrived appointing me to the joint Technical

Adjutant/Station Armament vacancy in Gibraltar with effect from 14 January 1948.

With Babs and Gina back at Brighton, I flew to Gibraltar by BEA Viking via refuelling stops at Bordeaux and Madrid, in those days a seven hour flight. Since my visits on the *Furious,* there had been a vast expansion of military facilities in defence against Hitler's plans to seize the fortress in 1940. The new runway jutting out to sea, built by the Canadian army, played a central role in the Allied invasion of N. Africa.

My duties included the disposal of stocks of wartime bombs and mines stored in caves inside the Rock linked by a labyrinth of tunnels. The honeycomb nature of the rock forming stalactites and stalagmites was not ideal for storage over a long period, and the bombs were exuding their high explosive content forming a dangerous encrustation. Rubber footwear was essential and no metal tools allowed during their hazardous transfer to the docks, for disposal at sea. Moorish Castle now a tourist attraction, was my pyrotechnic store, for which I held the keys.

Group Captain Walter Cheshire became the C.O. Born in St. Petersburg he spoke fluent Russian, and was Air Attaché in Moscow during the war.

Being unattached I was elected Mess Secretary and stood in for the President at a guest night dinner, on the occasion of a visit by Air Marshall Sir John Slessor and his American counterpart. The latter, after the first course, lit a Camel cigarette and I turned to Sir John on my left who smilingly said 'you're the President'. Thinking of what to say, there being no ashtrays provided prior to passing round the port, it had sunk in that it was out of order, and the cigarette extinguished.

Preparing the guest list for a VIP mess cocktail party entailed visits to Government House. The invitations included Prince Phillip, then 1st Lieutenant on *HMS Chequers*, his uncle Lord Louis Mountbatten, Admirals of the Home and Mediterranean fleets, Army and Air Force chiefs, local dignitaries and Sir Malcolm Sargent. Overseeing the preparations and accompanying the C.O. to formally greet the celebrities, was an anxious time, but thankfully all went well.

Pending allocation of a married quarter I booked accommodation at the Grand Hotel. Awaiting the arrival of the plane with Babs and Gina aboard, I was disappointed when, due to a cross-wind, it was unable to land and was diverted to Tangier. Their arrival next day, with Gina now six, scampering down the aircraft steps into my arms, followed by Babs, now pregnant again, is a joyful memory.

Our first floor suite had a large bay window and balcony, overlooking the busy cobbled Main Street, convenient for viewing such events as the daily Ceremony of the Keys. For this a troop of soldiers marched with a band to Casement Square where the ancient keys of the fortress were handed over to the Governor.

A short walk from the hotel was the Loretto Convent, where we arranged for Gina to attend the junior school.

On the 24 October 1949 I was scheduled to fly back to the UK to attend a Command HQ conference. My departure coincided with the arrival of *HMS Amethyst* on its daring escape from the Yangtze River incident. Whilst waiting to board the BEA Viking, I was approached by a Daily Telegraph reporter who stuffed a package of film in my tunic pocket, saying that I would be met on landing. Contact was made by Tannoy and I handed over the film. Next morning when the picture of the ship's arrival was published, I received a thank-you letter from the editor, including a Ten Pound cheque.

The mess squash court was a popular pastime where I once played Joshua Hassan, a local lawyer who became chief minister. He always insisted that Gibraltar would remain British as long as that was the wish of the majority of its residents.

We were allocated a flat in a married quarter block said to have been turned down for occupation by dockyard workers. Understandably so since there was no water on tap, our Spanish maid having to 'top-up' from a communal standpipe.

It was good to be with the RAF families to share the many spare time activities, such as swimming from Catalan Bay beach, and visiting the upper reaches of the Rock to mingle with the monkeys and view the magnificent mountains of Morocco across the Straits.

I took the opportunity to purchase a new Morris Minor, duty-free, for £310, the dealer Mr Gomez accepting post-dated cheques up to a year in settlement. It enabled us to escape the confinement of the Rock into the Spanish countryside, and the then peaceful fishing ports of La Linea and Algeciras, prior to their present expansion into holiday resorts.

I often wrote to Peggy to let the family know how Babs was getting along, and describing various aspects of our life on the Rock. She once replied sending me a copy of 'A Writers Notebook' by W. Somerset Maugham, and suggesting that I should 'take up the pen'. From someone so widely read, this was deeply encouraging, and I still have the book as a reminder.

Early in 1950 Babs was admitted to the military hospital for investigation of her heart condition. After several weeks it was decided that the pregnancy should be terminated. With the loss of a second child we were filled with grief, with little support, and reproof from the RC chaplain for my agreement to Babs' sterilization.

Arrangements were made for her to be invalided back home to the hospital at RAF Halton. I contacted Flt. Lt. Williams, now at the Air Ministry posting branch, who was able to meet my request, and I was appointed Adjutant of No. 2 Wing of the Apprentice School RAF Halton in the July. We travelled back to the UK by troopship with the usual turbulent crossing of the Bay of Biscay. The car was to follow in a Royal Navy vessel which was transporting Lord Mountbatten's polo ponies.

Disembarking on 26 May we stayed in London with Rosemary and Stefan in their spacious first floor flat in Bolton Gardens, pending the arrival of the car, which I collected from Portsmouth dockyard on 31 May, and visiting my parents in Lymington. The remainder of the four weeks overseas leave we spent at Ingatestone Hall, with visits to London and Brighton.

Leaving Gina with her cousin John and his nanny and Aunt Peggy, I drove Babs to Princess Mary's RAF Hospital at Halton in the vale of Aylesbury, Hertfordshire on 29 June. I took up residence in the officers' mess, once the country seat of Alfred Rothschild, the imposing staircase bearing his initials 'AR' in the wrought iron balustrade.

As wing adjutant it was strange to be leading the apprentices on the parade ground when I had not been accepted into their ranks. With their three years technical training they became the backbone of the Engineering Branch, twenty percent being commissioned and several, including Sir Frank Whittle, reaching air rank.

After one month Babs was discharged from hospital and although the assessment of her heart condition was inconclusive, it was considered sufficiently serious for it to be suggested that I retire from the RAF to look after her. At the age of thirty-four this was not financially feasible without some civilian employment. We therefore decided that I should carry on mindful that it may restrict my postings and promotion prospects.

With the apprentices' summer break starting, we collected Gina from Ingatestone, to spend three weeks by the sea, at Sussex Square in Brighton. Whilst there, I was unexpectedly notified of a posting to the Air Ministry in Kingsway in September 1950. Air Cdre. Chisman was now the Director of Air Servicing there, and once again I was to serve on his staff.

Now working in London, I stayed at Cissie's flat in Holland Park, visiting Babs and Gina in Brighton at weekends. It was a good opportunity to join the RAF Club at 128 Piccadilly, convenient for meeting colleagues and entertaining friends and relations, and visits to the club barber, Mr Reid. After a trim he singed the hair with a lighted taper, and then with Pomade Hongroise and heated tongs, modelled my military moustache. The latter, along with rolled umbrella, and raising my bowler on passing the Cenotaph, was no doubt why I always received a sword salute, to which I was entitled anyway, from the dismounted sentry at Horse Guards Parade.

Incidentally, the Silver Stick Adjutant of the Household Cavalry happened to be a namesake of mine, Capt. Clarence Piff. His duties in court circles were made use of by Eddie Crane, a former director of a finance company, who as an ex-wartime welfare officer used the rank of Captain and the Cavalry Club facilities. Reputedly a sparkling conversationalist and a brilliant host, and with Clarrie, who he claimed was his cousin, they entertained high society in sumptuous style at Sunning House in Sunningdale, which they rented from Lord Windlesham.

Peggy was once a guest there and mentioned to Clarrie that her brother-in-law had the same unusual surname. With such an opportune lead I had intended to contact him at the Cavalry Club, next door to the RAF Club, to discuss the family link. However, shortly afterwards, their names hit the headlines, Clarrie being declared bankrupt and resigning his commission, whilst Eddie went to prison for three years for fraud.

In January 1951 Babs and Gina left Brighton and we moved in with Rosemary and Stefan in Bolton Gardens, and arranged for Gina to attend the nearby Virgo Fidelis infant school. It was fortuitous that Air Cdre. Chisman was now Air Member of the Ordnance Board at Charles House, a new block of offices in Kensington, only a short walk from Bolton Gardens, and where I was to join him in March as his P.A., and as secretary of the inter-service Pyrotechnic Panel.

Things did not get off to a very good start with Babs being several weeks in the National Heart Hospital, whilst Gina suffered a severe attack of measles for which she was treated with injections. Though not noticeable at the time, the measles and/or the treatment brought about changes in her mental ability, which I shall refer to later.

Having been recommended for Staff College I went to the Air Ministry for an interview on 25 May and later learned that I had been accepted for No. 10 Course at RAF Andover starting on 28 April 1952.

Babs was again in hospital this time with jaundice for which she eventually had the gall bladder operation in Barts in the October.

My parents spent Christmas with the family in London, Eileen having recently moved to a flat in Brook Green, almost opposite the Queenshead. Taking them back to Lymington, accompanied by Babs and Gina, we stayed there over the New

Year, when I received the information that I had been promoted to Squadron Leader on 1st January 1952. On returning we travelled via Andover to Staines to visit Benny and Valerie, who he had married on 1 September 1949.

In preparation for Staff College I started a revision course of Pelmanism and attended seminars at the Institute of International Affairs, Chatham House, also making full use of my life membership of the Royal United Services Institute (R.U.S.I.) in Whitehall.

The Andover staff college re-opened after the war in the same hutted premises where it first started in 1922. No. 10 course was the last all-male entry, a third of whom were members of other air forces. Knowing there would be off-duty study involved, I decided to live in the mess for the twelve month duration of the course, as did the majority of the overseas students. We were split into small groups each with its own member of the directing staff under the commandant, Air. Cdre. Walter Cheshire, my C.O. in Gibraltar.

The intense studying was interspersed with course visits such as a week in the Newcastle area which included tours of Alnwick Castle, shipyards and steelworks, a trip down a coalmine, and finishing with a farewell function given by the Mayor in the civic centre.

I also recall exercise 'Shopwindow' at the RN base at Portsmouth where I experienced a cruise in the confined space of a submerged submarine. We visited Southwick House requisitioned during the war as HMS Dryad, the HQ of the Supreme Allied Commander Gen. Dwight D. Eisenhower, where he signalled the start of the invasion of Europe. After attending a quest night dinner at HMS Excellent, we stayed there overnight before returning to Andover.

The course assembled for lectures, many being given by eminent public figures and Service chiefs.

Being offered twice what I paid for it, I sold the Morris Minor, replacing it with a pre-war Riley 'Mentone' coachbuilt saloon, with a pre-selector gear lever on the steering wheel, for Eighty Pounds.

Rosemary and Stefan decided to emigrate to Buffalo USA, and Babs and Gina left Bolton Gardens in the August and moved back in with Mungar in Brighton.

Aircraft were available for the pilots on the course to keep in training and I often accompanied them in a dual control Anson or Proctor aircraft. My log book records a flight to the Royal Aircraft Establishment at Farnborough, to up-date myself on the research and development of armament equipment in preparation for a 'passing-out' lecture I was to give on the subject. Come the day, with my instructional experience at Manby, I was fairly confident and the allocated forty-five minutes on the rostrum went in a flash, followed by a fifteen minute break for coffee which I shared with the Commandant in his office. Commenting on my performance he implied that I had been hiding my light under a bushel. Returning for question time I was now even more confident, and was complimented by the Directing Staff.

A course visit to the staff college at Bracknell was arranged for a debating session to be followed by a formal dinner, for which we were wearing mess kit. On arrival a message awaited me that Gina had been admitted to the Royal Sussex Hospital for an operation to remove an abscess in her neck, previously incorrectly diagnosed as mumps. With the Commandants' permission, I left immediately and made my way by train to Brighton and the hospital. The operation was successful and when she fully recovered we arranged for her to attend school at the Sacred Heart Convent in Hove, where her cousins, Eileen's daughters Jacqueline and Christine were also boarders.

We spent Christmas with Peggy at her new abode in North Stoke, she and Joe having decided to live apart. Atty Corbett the son of Lord Rowallan was an amateur steeplechase jockey, who later became a racehorse trainer, also lived there as a base for his racing pursuits.

In the New Year, the final stages of the course included the writing of a thesis on a chosen subject, mine being 'Unification of the Armed Forces' which has always intrigued me since my time on the *Furious*, along with Lord Trenchards dictum of the 'Indivisibility of Air Power'. I submitted it under the title 'Tria Juncta in Uno', and it was later returned with two pages of hand written comments from the Commandant, the final sentence saying 'Your thesis is well written and arranged, I have found it both interesting and stimulating, excellent work'.

Since then, although the Admiralty, War Office and Air Ministry have been combined into a Ministry of Defence, the Army and Navy still control their own aircraft, and each have separate soldiers in the form of the Royal Marines and the RAF Regiment, while the Air Force and Army both operate some marine craft.

A farewell guest night was held on 20 March to which I invited Babs and Peggy. Sam Weller a course colleague being unaccompanied, partnered Peggy, and with two other couples at our table it was the most light-hearted and enjoyable meal I remember. After dinner it was remarkable how Peggy's personality attracted such attention, especially from those interested in racing.

The course assembled for a final address by the Chief of the Air Staff Sir William Dickson in which he quoted another of Trenchard's maxims 'the role of the staff officer is to continually seek more and more operational capability for less and less money', precisely the aim of my thesis.

At the farewell interview, having successfully passed the course, I was awarded the letters p.s.c. to appear after my name in the Air Force list, a satisfying present for my thirty seventh birthday, and a good start for my appointment as Group Armament Officer at 12 Group HQ, RAF Newton, after Easter.

Prior to taking up my new appointment I visited the Command Armament Officer, Gp. Capt. Harding and his deputy Sqn. Ldr. John Palmer at HQ Fighter Command, Stanmore. I was surprised at the large number of Units in East Anglia and the North comprising No. 12 Group, and which I would need to visit. An improvement in the fixed gun stoppage rate was to be my main concern.

On my way to RAF Newton near Nottingham, I stopped in Blisworth where my father spent his childhood, and then into Northampton to visit his sister's daughter, my cousin Dorothy and husband Cecil. Their married daughter Maureen lived at Burton Joyce, just across the river in Nottingham, so we frequently met, and have since kept in touch.

Musters Court, a block of flats in West Bridgford, had been requisitioned for officer married quarters, and Sgn. Ldr. Bob Sergeant who lived there invited me for coffee to view the place and meet his wife Vicky. Overlooking Trent Bridge cricket ground on the outskirts of Nottingham, and a short drive to the office, it was very suitable, especially as Babs would be in touch with the other wives, whilst I was away on my visits. I put my name on the waiting list and we eventually moved into one of the first floor flats.

On Coronation Day 2 June 1953, I had reserved tickets at the RUSI Whitehall to view the royal procession. As Peggy and John were to attend the actual ceremony in Westminster Abbey, we arranged to take them there on our way. To make an early start and avoid the traffic, we all stayed the previous night at Eileen's flat in Brook Green. With the frivolity of that evening, I had forgotten to 'top-up' the car, and we came to a halt on the Embankment. I felt Peggy could have hit me with her handbag, but I hailed a taxi for her and John, and went in search of a garage. By the time I returned carrying a can of petrol in full service dress, and on our way again, the traffic was building-up. Whilst stuck in a traffic jam Babs decided she had 'had enough', and I saw her off back to Eileen's by taxi. Gina and I eventually reached Whitehall, and took up our seats at a window in the Banqueting Hall with its famous Ruben painted ceiling, where we had a first class view of the Royal procession.

A Communication Flight was based at Newton which I frequently used to reduce travelling time on staff visits. On

4 December 1953 I flew to Acklington in an Anson to visit a squadron at the practice camp, having difficulty with their gun stoppage rate. The pilot W.O. Yearsley-Struthers came to see me after lunch to ask if I would leave earlier than planned, as the weather was closing-in. I had to weigh-up the need to make a return visit, or to finish the work in hand, and go back by train. Luckily I decided the latter for the pilot and passengers were killed when, due to engine failure on the approach at Newton, the plane somersaulted and landed upside down on the runway. My telephone call to Babs about my delayed return was not until after the tragic news had reached Musters Court, but fortunately Vicky was with her to share the shock.

In the New Year Bob was posted overseas to Kuala Lumpur on 1 March leaving Vicky and young son Michael to join him later. Meanwhile she was good company for Babs before bidding her parents in Fulham farewell prior to embarking in *SS Empire Orwell* on 14 April. Eileen's husband Wag was aboard at the same time on an army posting to Korea.

Once when in London walking down Pall Mall, I met Sqn. Ldr. Simpson who I had served under at Manby and Morpeth. No longer in the RAF he was now a 'high flyer' in the City, and he invited me to lunch at Simpsons in the Strand.

I replaced the Riley with a new Ford Popular which being a basic model, had no heating and on long distance visits in winter I was frozen stiff. Staff visits became less widespread with the formation of No. 13 Group under Air Cdre. W. Cheshire, to take over the Northern section.

In November Benny and Val were back from Hong Kong for a spell of language study of the local lingo at University, before returning the following March. We invited them to the pre-Christmas mess ball, along with Maureen and husband Fred (p.143). After introducing them on arrival, to the Unit CO Sqn. Ldr. Bob Pugh and wife Sheila, Babs was not feeling well and I took her home, but she insisted I returned to be with our guests.

We spent Christmas with Peggy at North Stoke, along with Mungar and Sarah who, aged 4, made it inevitable that I had to dress-up and play the role of Santa Claus. Earlier that year Atty had won the Mildmay Chase, and the prestigious prize presented by the Queen, had pride of place on the dining room mantelpiece. After Christmas, Peggy took Gina and John to visit the Earl of Carnarvon at Highclere for a tea party and fireworks at his son Lord Porchester's house by the lakeside.

Later in the year, nearing completion of my time at 12 Group, I was notified of a posting to the Royal Aircraft Establishment at Farnborough. No particular appointment being specified, I did not know what would be involved, so Babs and our belongings went to Brighton for the time being, and I arrived in Farnborough on 27 November 1955.

I moved into the hutted accommodation of the No. 1 Officers Mess it being the first when the Royal Air Force was formed in 1918 under Lord Trenchard whose HQ, in an adjacent building, Trenchard House, is now the Air Science Museum. My room overlooked the airfield where in 1908 Col. S. F. Cody made the first officially recorded flight in Great Britain, commemorated with a plaque on the preserved remnants of the tree to which he tethered his aircraft.

US/UK atomic weapon collaboration had ceased after WW2 but in March 1955 President Eisenhower had announced that tactical atomic weapons would be available to contain any Russian aggression in Europe. I was to join a civilian team to design and air test the necessary installation for this capability in the Canberra, prior to its eventual provision for squadrons in 2nd TAF.

I was involved in all aspects including participating in test flights, taking minutes of meetings, recording results and progress, in order to draft the final report.

We kept in close contact with the main contractor ML Aviation (Mobbs and Labelle). The latter an interesting Belgian character, was a frequent visitor often taking Dave

King, the team leader, and myself to lunch in his Bentley to the Bell and Dragon at Crookham or the Waterside Inn at Bray.

Knowing I was looking for married accommodation, Johnny Palmer, now at Farnborough, told me about a flat which had become vacant, conveniently near the RAE North Gate, and we went along to view. It was a three bedroom ground floor maisonette, in a modern black of four flats, in over an acre known as Highbury Close, between the Farnborough College of Technology and its seldom used sports field, in the unmade-up Boundary Road. I quickly obtained the tenancy and we moved in just before Christmas 1955, only three weeks after my arrival. It was the start of a long friendship over the years with Johnny and his wife Vera, daughter Marion and son Barry.

Once whilst my parents were staying with us, Peggy called in and took us all to tea at Eton, where John was now at the college. I took Gina to the Fourth of June celebrations there that year and had to leave her with John until his parents arrived, whilst I attended a meeting at the Air Ministry. Returning in the afternoon I was in time for the riverside picnic on Agars Plough and the boating and firework display. I also remember on other occasions, the lavish contents of that hamper from the boot of Joe's Rolls Royce

The September SBAC Air Show was a busy week entertaining visitors in the mess, an ideal place to watch the flying display. One afternoon I was entertaining the USAAF officers and their wives when they were unexpectedly called away to their HQ in Ruislip, and I was left with the five females until their return.

Usually on Sundays we went to High Mass at St Michaels Abbey built in French Gothic and Romanesque style for the Empress Eugenie, as a mausoleum for Napoleon III and their son, alongside the ancient monastery of Benedictine monks. The Empress lived at Farnborough Hill, now a convent girl's school.

With the advantage of its location, near the A30 between London and Lymington, I successfully negotiated the purchase of the freehold flat, setting my sights on acquiring the other three and further developing the extensive plot. Removing one of the buttressed walls of the fives court provided a drive-in entrance to a temporary car port for the A30 Austin estate car, a recent replacement for the Ford.

Through Peggy's contacts, Babs was now attending a consultant at the London Clinic who, whilst treating her for a heart condition, referred her to a psychiatrist regarding her reactions to the symptoms. For this she was admitted to the North Middlesex Hospital, and although she came home at week-ends, she was not discharged until after three months.

The project was going according to plan, and thinking of the need to practice the release manoeuvre at squadron level, I designed an attachment to enable the standard RAF practice bombs to be used for training purposes. A prototype was manufactured by Portsmouth Aviation and after trials, a supply order was placed.

For Christmas 1957 we again gathered at Ingatestone Hall, joined by Joe's cousin Nicky Throckmorton. His ancestor Sir John Throckmorton had been active in denouncing anti-Catholicism at the time of the Gordon Riots when Lord Petre's London house was sacked prior to the Emancipation Act of 1829. Whilst there I had the memorable experience of participating in a large organised shooting party, with beaters and dogs.

The project trials now completed, I had submitted the draft report, and in May I was notified of my posting as O.C. Technical Wing with the rank of Wing Commander, at RAF Stradishall, a Fighter Command station in Suffolk, with effect from 30 June 1958.

I did not receive a particularly warm welcome from Gp. Capt. D. Lister, the station commander at Stradishall, who had misgivings about a weapons specialist being in charge of the servicing and maintenance of the different jet aircraft of the three fighter squadrons. Placing me on a month's trial I had to break the news to him that the Air Ministry, when appointing me, had sanctioned my imminent three weeks leave overseas already booked, which did not enhance my position.

Gina and I were to join Peggy and John on a drive to Amalfi in her open tourer via the South of France, and to visit Capri. Babs not being well enough, stayed with Mungar. It was a great holiday which set me up to tackle the task confronting me.

We were allotted an eight bedroom married quarter, used as a WAAF officers mess during the war, with large gardens, an enormous kitchen with butlers pantry, and sited next to the C.O.'s house. Fortunately for Babs, a civilan batman took care of the housework, and stoked the basement boiler, before bringing us an early morning cup of tea.

Being in charge of over a thousand airmen involved a considerable amount of administration in addition to supervision of the aircraft maintenance. However, serviceability targets were being met, credit due to the core of Halton trained tradesmen. Before leaving, the C.O. had overcome his doubts about me taking over, and invited me to join him in a dual Meteor 7 on a visit to Martlesham Heath.

The station seemed to 'light-up' with the arrival of his replacement, the pipe-smoking Gp. Capt. Christopher Foxley-Norris, DSO. Ex Winchester and Oxford, where he and his long time friend Leonard Cheshire (the future Gp. Capt. Lord Cheshire VC), were members of the University Air Squadron. His commencement of a career at the Bar coincided with the outbreak of the war, and he became a Battle of Britain fighter pilot. Then aged twenty-two he wrote the following verse which was read out by Archbishop Dr. Runcie in Westminster Abbey at the fiftieth Battle of Britain anniversary:

A common unconsidered man
Who for a moment of eternity
Held the whole future of mankind
In his two sweating palms
And did not let it go.

As chairman of the Battle of Britain Association, he publicly criticised the then Prime Minister Tony Blair for not replying to, let alone accepting, an invitation to attend the sixtieth service of commemoration.

Group Captain L. Cheshire (Ret'd) had recently married Sue Ryder and living in nearby Cavendish, they frequently visited the C.O. and his wife Joan. After his retirement as Air Chief Marshall Sir Christopher Foxley-Norris DSO, GCB he became president of the Cheshire Foundation providing homes for the disabled in forty-five countries.

We made good use of the spare rooms for guests including my mother and father. Peggy's visit for a mess ball, where meeting the fighter pilots and next day joining them for lunch-time drinks in the Cherry Tree, reminded her of her pre-war links with 601 Squadron. Joe visited in his Rolls in which after lunch, I took him on a tour of the airfield and squadrons, and Atty Corbett discovered we were a convenient base for the Newmarket races.

Vicky and Bob, now back from the Far East were at Horsham St Faith, Norwich, and came to stay for a cocktail party in the mess which they knew well, having previously been stationed here.

The annual open-day for the public included a flying display and I invited Wg. Cmdr. Ken Wallis, the Command Armament Officer, to take part in his self-built auto-giro (p.144), which he brought towed behind his car. The short forty five degree take-off made one wonder whether it would fulfil Henry Fords forecast, that such means of conveyance would one day replace the car. He constructed sixteen versions of the machine, broke twenty world records, and after a demonstration at Pinewood Studios, he was written into the James Bond film 'You Only Live Twice'. Aged ninety he was still flying when a freak wind caused him to crash land into goal posts on a sports field, and was reported in the press.

Local residents from adjoining country houses were invited to mess functions, notably Brigadier Frink (Ret'd) and his wife, whose daughter Elizabeth was the remarkably gifted sculptress.

My father's health had been failing and he was admitted to Lyminton Hospital where he died on 4 November 1959 aged 79.

In 1960 Gp. Capt. Foxley-Norris left to take over RAF West Malling, in need of his lively leadership. After a short while he rang to ask me to visit to advise him on the organisation of the Technical Wing. I was able to highlight some necessary changes, and thanking me he mentioned that I had further to go in my RAF career.

He was replaced by Gp. Capt. Stan Grant DFC a former Spitfire pilot who in 1942, as CO of 249 Squadron in the defence of Malta, dealt a severe blow to the German and Italian air forces, for which he was awarded the DFC and Bar.

I had booked for us, accompanied by Peggy and John to go on a skiing holiday in Zermatt, Switzerland, with the RAF Winter Sports Association, but it was cancelled when Babs was admitted to the RAF Hospital at Ely for further investigation, which again was inconclusive.

Eileen, now divorced, married Major F. Robins REME, (Ret'd), on 23 January 1960, and took over the historic Eagle Hotel opposite Kings College Chapel in Cambridge. The bar ceiling covered with USAAF and RAF signatures, was a relic of its wartime connections.

Approaching the end of my tour of duty I was notified of a posting to the Ministry of Aviation in London on 30 May 1960 dealing with the safety aspects of guided weapons, and as Chairman of the Electrical Explosive Hazard Committee.

Farnborough being only half an hour by train to Waterloo, we moved into our flat there having arranged for it to be vacated, and we arrived with our belongings packed into the A30 estate car. This I later traded in for a Vauxhall Victor in which our first drive was to collect Gina from the convent at the end of her last term, with the three of us sitting on the bench-type front seat. She had stayed for an extra year and her final report mentioned her difficulty in concentrating, whilst her manners and conduct were very good. She had been seen by Madame Orgler a psychologist who visited the school, and being an advocate of her fellow countryman Alfred Adler, after several sessions diagnosed an 'inferiority complex'. This if anything was a symptom rather than a cause, but in all fairness, little was known at the time about the different forms of autism and its connection with measles. This I am reasonably sure was when the problem began, and like many others so afflicted, she has a razor like memory of dates and peoples names.

During our absence the layout of Farnborough had changed with the construction of dual carriageways, roundabouts, a new shopping area, and Boundary Road was now built-up, no longer a footpath into the woods.

My job entailed many staff visits to other establishments and manufacturers whose representatives frequently came to report progress and take me out to lunch in some exclusive restaurants such as Rules in Maiden Lane and the Waldorf Hotel, where its new owner, Charles Forte, was once sitting at the next table.

In August 1960 Babs was in the Cambridge Military Hospital in Aldershot when I received a telegram marked with a red label 'Government Absolute Priority'. Panic set in as I was opening it, fortunately to find that she had been removed from the 'seriously ill list'.

Gina attended a grooming and deportment course at Lucie Claytons in New Bond Street, a finishing school founded in 1928, and she was assessed as 'above average'.

The following May Mungar came to stay with Babs whilst I took Gina to Paris by air to visit John, now at the Sorbonne. One night I took them to the Crazy Horse night club where the stage show was rather risqué, but Gina was now eighteen and John a year older. On the Sunday, Peggy met us for lunch at the George V Hotel, one of the three Parisian hotels later owned by Charles Forte.

In November 1961 I set off on a three week visit to Adelaide for duty at the Woomera rocket range. Flying in a DC6 charter flight took us five days, stopping at Benina, Aden, Colombo, Singapore and Darwin. Whilst in Colombo a fellow passenger, Wg. Cdr. Joe Adey asked if I would like to accompany him to meet his wartime associate Arthur C. Clarke who now lived here on the coast. En route to the beachside bungalow in an open taxi I learnt a little about his background in the RAF when he specialised in RADAR, and in 1945 still in his twenties, he made his visionary predictions in a famous article on the future of world communications, and later his far reaching achievements in this direction using satellites.

When we arrived he was playing table tennis with three spry Sinhalese lads with whom he had been scuba diving. Whilst he and Joe Adey were reminiscing I played 'ping-pong' with the boys and later I also played our host, and lost. I was not altogether surprised when many years later, newspapers reported the postponement of his investiture for a Knighthood, mentioning the reputation of the area as being a haven for paedophiles. He refuted any such allegations and eventually received the award in May 2000 honouring his title as 'father of satellite communications', and his eminence as a science fiction writer.

My stay in Adelaide coincided with John Betjeman's Antipodean tour and I attended a well applauded presentation he gave of his writings, in the crowded city hall. It seemed to fit the time warp feeling I had about the place, with threepenny bits still in circulation, teenage schoolboys in short trousers and school caps, and families attending church in their Sunday best clothes.

Wishfully thinking that Gina was growing out of her immaturity, we entered her for a Pitman's secretarial course. After a short while we received a letter to the effect that she could not continue being unable to cope with the syllabus, and recommending that her ability be tested. The need for this was highlighted when on a staff visit to Horsham St Faith, I took Gina with me having arranged to leave her with Vicky at their married quarter whilst I was busy. Vicky not having seen her for over two years the immaturity was more noticeable, and she made this known to me.

I made an appointment for Gina to see Dr Dicks in Wimpole Street for testing over two days. He sent a full page report and though specifying a border-line I.Q. he stressed that on the positive side she was reliable and trustworthy and would be capable of repetitive type employment.

I was offered an eighteen months appointment as C.O. of a maintenance unit in Aden and though tempted by it being a step to promotion, I declined bearing Babs needs in mind. Instead I was to become Command Armament Officer at HQ Fighter Command on 27 May 1963.

We moved into a large married quarter in Beamish Drive, Bushey Heath, within walking distance from my office in the 18th century Bentley Priory. Surprisingly I met Bob who was now in the Air Staff here and occupying a married quarter near ours. Their son Michael was shortly to leave for Rhodesia to join the British South African police.

Gina was assessed by the Social Services who found her to be suitable to fill a vacancy as a ward assistant at the Shrodell Hospital in Watford, only a short bus ride when I was unable to take her by car.

I was frequently away on staff visits flying from RAF Bovingdon, including a trip to the attachments in Germany and to Le Bourget for the 1965 Paris air show. It amounted to a total of thirty seven flights in two years.

During my absence it was a relief to know that Vicky was nearby to help Babs, and consequently it was not good news when Bob was posted in April 1964. Vicky however decided to stay behind and on vacating their married quarter, she moved in with us, which was a great help to Babs, though it must have seemed like a ménage à trois.

She joined us for mass each Sunday, and deciding to become a Catholic she underwent instruction from the parish priest Fr. Stephen Rigley, who baptised her on 11 August 1964.

The following year I was notified of a move back to the Ministry of Aviation in London and being within commuting distance we were allowed to remain in the married quarter. I was now serving under Gp. Capt. 'Lofty' Webber, the Assistant Director of Air Armament.

Later, the Ministry of Aviation became the Ministry of Technology and I was moved to the Guided Weapons section dealing with the propulsion and warheads of new weapons under development.

The owner of the flat above ours in Farnborough was moving and my offer to buy it was accepted. As I frequently visited the R.A.E. on duty, it was a good opportunity to move back there once again, Vicky agreeing to occupy the newly acquired flat above.

Babs' walking had become unsteady and a wheelchair was now a help in getting her out and about. We often went to Southsea to visit Vicky's widowed mother who lived on the front, and whose brother and sister, Bill and Gladys, who shared a house nearby. We also went to see Peggy, now living in Newmarket, where she later became Mayor.

Following an appointment with Dr Graham Hayward, Babs was again admitted to Barts. I visited her each day and on the 8th August 1967 I stayed with her most of the afternoon. At midnight the ward sister rang me with the tragic news that my wife had died at 11.30pm. I lay awake all night full of anguish and worrying about what had to be done in the next few days, notifying relatives and friends, collecting her affects from the hospital and death certificate from the Guildhall, arranging the funeral. With Gina I visited Mungar who was staying with Sarah in Peggy's London house in Queensdale Road.

Although having been treated for a heart condition, the autopsy revealed that Babs had suffered the symptoms of Multiple Sclerosis, a progressive disease of the central nervous system. Little was then known about it whilst now about fifty, mostly women aged between twenty and forty, are diagnosed with the complaint every week. There is no known cause or cure for MS. Its symptoms strike without warning and include loss of mobility, slurred speech, fatigue and depression.

The funeral took place on 14 August with requiem mass at Brook Green with Charles as M.C., followed by internment at Mortlake, well attended by relatives and friends.

Feeling I had to get away for a few days, I arranged for Gina to stay at a holiday care home at Hayling Island, whilst I went on a duty visit at Weston-Super-Mare. On the way back I spent three days leave in Melksham with Benny and Val where they now ran an antique shop. In the meantime Vicky was holding the fort at Farnborough with her mother keeping her company.

I was now looking ahead regarding my next and final appointment. Being in the rank of Wing Commander for ten years and now unaccompanied, I was prepared to forego possible promotion in favour of returning to the R.A.E. to settle in Farnborough and plan my retirement. After putting out the usual feelers it transpired that a guided weapons post there would be available in the New Year, and my application was accepted.

Back at the R.A.E. on 28 March 1968, I joined a team dealing with the development of Martel the Anglo-French guided weapon. The name is derived from Missile Anti-Radar and Television. The T.V. version, with which I was involved, had a camera in the nose to transmit a picture of the target area on to a screen in the aircraft so that adjustments could be made to obtain a direct hit.

My office in 134 building was near the North Gate opposite the top end of Boundary Road, and close to the officers' mess. Gina's new place of work, the local War Memorial Cottage Hospital, was also nearby.

Thankfully Vicky continued to do the housekeeping and although now separated from Bob for over two years, it was still a shock when he started divorce proceedings preparatory to marrying a WRAF officer.

During a visit by the Prince of Wales and the Duke of Edinburgh, I was manning the Martel exhibition in which they took a good deal of interest. I again met the Duke at a royal cocktail party which the Queen and he attended at the RAF club. Mike Beetham, a fellow student at staff college, now Air Commodore, was officiating. He had broken several jet aircraft endurance records, and was on his way to later become Marshal of the Royal Air Force.

Whilst watching the 1968 SBAC air show with Benny and Val, the C.O. Gp. Capt. Morrison called me aside to say he was appointing me to take over as President of the Mess Committee. Being the No. 1 mess, I felt honoured that my name would be added to the fifty year old list of previous presidents, displayed in the entrance.

At last I purchased the remaining two flats and now owned the extensive site. My sister Cissie, her husband having died the previous year, was soon to retire from a long spell at Selfridges, moved into a ground floor flat. She later became a receptionist at the local Jenner House surgery where Wg.

Cdr. David Urquhart (Ret'd), formerly at the Institute of Aviation Medicine, and a mess member, was now practicing. On her eightieth birthday he held a celebration in his house with a host of friends and relatives. The upper flat was let to an RAE civilian staff member chosen from a long list of applicants.

Vicky, now divorced, having given such stalwart support over the years, we understandably had grown very close and became engaged. Contemplating a R.C. church wedding it was necessary to submit a petition to Rome on account of Vicky's previous marriage. Doubtful about it being sanctioned after waiting several months, we married in a registry office on 25 January 1969, and had a celebratory lunch with a few relatives at the Berystede Hotel, Sunninghill. We then drove off on honeymoon without Vicky knowing our destination until we arrived at the Savoy Hotel, where a luxury suite bedecked with flowers, and overlooking the river, awaited us.

Belatedly, a reply arrived from the Diocesan Tribunal to the effect that as there was no record of Vicky having been baptised before her former marriage, our petition was granted, and a church blessing of the marriage took place.

My brother Charles had been admitted to Charing Cross Hospital for investigation of a bronchial disorder. It being untreatable he was transferred to Twyford Abbey hospice, and his son Christopher with Cissie and I where at his bedside when he died there from lung cancer on 25 March 1969, aged 63.

My duties necessitated several visits to Paris and in March 1970 I took Vicky with me to spend four days on leave there. She also accompanied me at the top table for guest night dinners, and once when leading the members and guests into the dining hall, the Royal Marine band started playing 'Those Magnificent Men in Their Flying Machines'.

Approaching the end of my RAF career I received a Charter Scroll from the Council of Engineering Institutions which states:-

'By virtue of his academic qualifications, professional training and experience –
Reginald Edward George PIFF
Has upon the nomination of the Royal Aeronautical Society
Been registered by the Council and is hereby authorised to
Use the style and title of 'CHARTERED ENGINEER'.
Dated 3rd day of November 1970.'

My spare time was spent designing our dream house to be built alongside the block of flats, and I submitted the proposed property for planning permission. This was granted and I gave my drawings to the family firm of local builders Hilder and Son, established in 1922. Site preparation began in October 1969 and Major Hilder nearly eighty, put his son Howard in charge.

Along with the traditional workmanship, roof trusses being made on site for example, with which I was very impressed, there were delays due to late ordering of materials, and it was ten months before we moved in. As 'back of an envelope' type accounting and lack of business control was the cause, Major Hilder asked if I would consider joining the firm on my retirement, to cover this aspect. Having accepted, I chose a four week 'bricks and mortar' resettlement course in Aldershot prior to my release leave. I retired on 11 April 1971 on completing thirty seven years in the RAF, serving under four monarchs and with eleven prime ministers; the year that the Armed Forces Act discontinued the future use of the term 'officer and a gentleman'.

Babs at Arosa - 1939

Peggy and Babs at their sister Rosemary's wedding - 1947 with Mungar

The avenue of trees in our garden at Boundary Road Farnborough

With Maureen and Fred, Valerie and brother Benny at a Mess Ball RAF Newton - 1954

Wg. Cdr. Ken Wallis in his Auto gino - RAF Stradishall - 1959

Meeting up with Vicky after Gina and I attended a Royal Garden party - July 1968

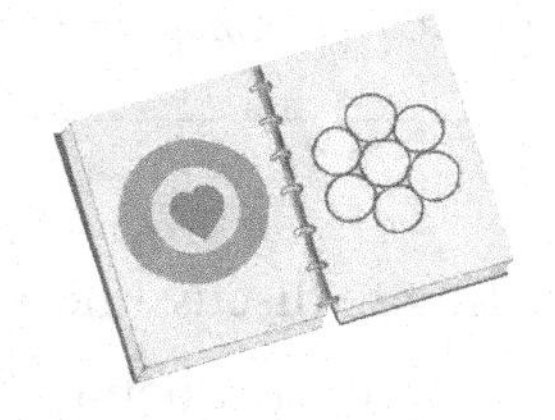

CHAPTER 4

(1971-1983) 'Out of the Blue'

Now with 'Hilder the builder' my first task was to tackle the backlog of paperwork in the office in Hilder Gardens, a cul-de-sac of large houses which the firm had developed. To reconcile the outstanding bank statements, I started a double-entry cash book, much to the relief of the accountant on a brief visit.

Hutted workshops where tools and materials were stored, stood on the large Pinehurst site, owned by Hilder, in the centre of Farnborough where a weekly market was held. Negotiations for the Council to acquire the site were completed with a large recently built factory for the firm, as part of the deal. With offices on the ground and first floors, it was not necessary for a house builder.

However, Mr Vaux the bank manager, considering expansion in other directions, contacted the financial consultants

I.C.F.C. A senior executive arranged a meeting to discuss the matter over lunch at the Queen's Hotel, but Howard being otherwise engaged asked me to stand in for him. After a lengthy session giving a favourable account of the firm, and an assurance that I would involve myself in the expansion, the wheels were quickly set in motion.

It had already been arranged for Richard Twite an architect, to deal with design and layout, which Major Hilder had formerly managed. Also the quick-build advantage of timber frame housing was realised, involving co-operation with Yorkshire Homes, the suppliers.

The team of I.C.F.C. consultants set themselves up in the factory offices, whilst examining our present commitments, and exploring feasible expansion. Their recommendations resulted in setting up a Building Design Centre comprising five limited companies of which I was to be the Group Administration Manager.

The necessary machinery was installed in the factory for the construction of kitchen and bathroom furniture, and office staff and additional tradesmen employed. The staff cars included Howard's Landrover and mine, a new Ford Cortina.

A show house was built on the factory site which served as the design office. Such was the progress, that a further show house, opened to the public by the comedian Eric

Morecombe, was displayed at the Ideal Home Exhibition at Olympia in March 1973.

Unfortunately with the economic crisis of 1974, there was a sudden slump in the housing market. Now with a surplus of sites and unsold properties, I accompanied Howard and Mr Vaux to a meeting at the group office of the bank in Guildford. The decision was made to close the companies down and enter into liquidation proceedings with the official receiver.

Staff were discharged and I was re-employed by the receiver for the winding down period, and I was permitted to purchase the company car. It was a busy period as apart from holding the keys to the factory and the unsold properties, I was in constant contact with estate agents for valuations and viewings. Also I had to attend creditors meetings and deal with the closure of company accounts at the receiver's office in the City. Here the same office block housed the headquarters of the Wm. Hudson Corporation of which Sqn. Ldr. Lindsay Simpson was now chairman, but unfortunately I failed to contact him.

During these three years of business activity, much had occurred on the home front. My mother was admitted to Courtaulds Hospital in Braintree where she died on 13 June 1972, aged 92. I arranged for the funeral to take place in Lymington where my father was buried.

The following year Eileen's husband died and we attended the funeral with Christopher, in Appledore where they had retired to after eight years at the Eagle in Cambridge.

Family members being widely dispersed, there was much travelling on frequent visits. Also as a volunteer for the RAF Benevolent Fund, I attended meetings at various locations, and visited clients. Most summers we went to West Bexington staying in a beach bungalow on Chesil Bank, 'far from the madding crowd'.

In September 1974 the local hospital was closed down and the staff including Gina, were transferred to the new one at Frimley Park.

The following summer we attended a royal garden party at Buckingham Palace, just two days before Vicky went to New Zealand on a months visit to her well-travelled son.

A spare time hobby was tracing my branch of the family tree. There was no computer facility for this at the time, and it entailed many trips to the Records Office in London. I also visited Piffs Elm, a hamlet in the parish of Elmstone Hardwicke between Tewkesbury and Cheltenham, so named when a twenty foot girth tree, which until 1844 stood in front of the White Swan, a coaching inn run by several generations of my ancestors. Making notes of Piffs buried in the churchyard, and imbibing a local brew labelled 'Piffs Perfidy' in the inn, now known as the Gloucester Old Spot, I eventually compiled a lineage of nine generations.

Later I wrote an article 'Piffs Elm – A family Tree' published in the Family Tree Magazine November 1999. Pending the perusal of possible progenitorial connections on the Continent, it concluded 'the deeper roots of the family tree must rest with those of that memorable elm, the stump of which still remains in that once secluded corner of the Cotswolds'.

I often wonder why Charles Dickens (1812-1870) used the name of Piff for characters in two of his tales – Miss Piff in 'Mugby Junction', and Mrs Piff in the 'Runaways', mindful of his visits to his friend Macready in this part of Gloucestershire, which is the location for several of his major stories.

It is also known that he based several characters on his ex-mistresses e.g. Dora in 'David Copperfield' and Maria in 'Little Dorrit'. Aware of this procilivity and the striking resemblance between his portrait once depicted on the ten pound note, and that of my grandfather Charles Piff b. Cheltenham 1851, makes me ponder the possibility of my being of Dickensian descent, perchance a prosaist protégé.

Once whilst staying with us, Vicky's mother, Mabel Brookes, strolled into the Knellwood War Memorial Home, a large country house at the bottom of Boundary Road. Being favourably impressed and so near to her daughter, she became a resident and moved there from Southsea in January 1978. With Vicky visiting to help with the tea trolley and play the piano, she was very happy, but sadly suddenly died there in November 1979. The home which I shall refer to later, has since been extensively enlarged.

In 1978 I was undergoing treatment for nocturnal epilepsy. Although a CAT brain scan at the Atkinson Morley Hospital in London was normal, and Epanutin tablets were proving to be effective, I was banned from driving for twelve months. I sold the Cortina replacing it with a new Maxi B2 in July 1979.

That year I was admitted to the St Thomas Hospital, Ward 10 overlooking the Thames, for a kidney biopsy under an epidural spinal anaesthetic. The urological disorder being investigated, swollen ankles, was successfully treated with medication.

The sale of 37 Gunterstone Road enabled me to pay off the mortgages on the block of flats in Farnborough, the loan rate then being 10.5%. It also covered the cost of renewing the window frames, re-surfacing the flat roof, and new guttering. Architects plans for two additional second floor flats were approved but in view of the above repair work, I fortunately as you will see, put the matter on hold.

The tenants, apart from my sister, were mainly RAE staff including Francis Wilson, now a TV weather forecaster. When he left and the flat above became vacant, I arranged for Gina and four of her similarly placed colleagues to move in, and be supervised by a social worker.

Management of the college bookshop where Vicky was helping became available and we took it on, signing the contract on 1 September 1980. It was quite interesting and profitable though time consuming, dealing with the accounts, progressing orders, visiting publishers, and manning the shop during the day and evening sessions. The long holiday breaks however allowed us to take the car to Jersey, and one Christmas we flew to Malta staying at the Phoenicia Hotel in Valetta.

The college had a branch at Manor Park in Aldershot where it was decided that the bookshop facilities were also needed. We transported the necessary stock and set up shop for evening sessions.

We bought a 3-speed Honda mower for the large areas of lawns, the cuttings being composted in two six foot square crates. These produced a rich fertilizer when mixed with the daily clearance of the chicken hutch I had constructed for a clutch of cackling hens. The latter were reluctantly disposed of, there now being insufficient time to tend them. With the regular raking of leaf-fall in the autumn it was all becoming somewhat exhausting.

Then in December 1982 Mr Galloway, the Hampshire County Council architect visited me with an aerial photograph showing my site between the college and the sports field, to discuss the proposal to extend the college. The outcome of this after my three months in hospital (Chapter 1) is covered in the following chapters.

Attending a Royal Garden Party - 1985

With Vicky at a Mess Ball - RAF officers Mess, Farnborough - 1970

Ingatestone Hall, Essex

Knellwood, Canlerbury Road Farnborough, Hants

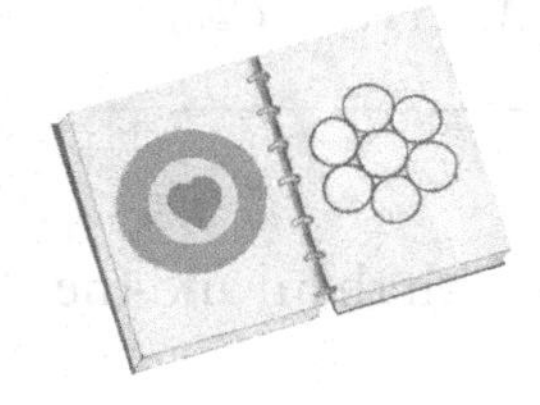

Chapter 5

(1983-2003) 'The Aftermath'

As advised by the hospital I put my feet up after lunch, as my dear mother used to, referring to it as 'having forty winks'. This compensated for me only sleeping six to seven hours at night, having got into the habit of waking at 5.30am to tune into Radio 4's 'UK Theme', a good start to the day, until it was discontinued after 33 years.

The sale of the Boundary Road site for the extension of the college having been settled, a meeting was arranged on 4 May 1983 to discuss a time scale for vacation of the properties for demolition. Cissie's son Michael purchased a flat for her in Highgate Court, conveniently near Farnborough station, as she continued commuting to Selfridges until 1988.

A detached five bedroom house nearby, with a bus stop outside, seemed fitting for Gina and the girls, subject to some refurbishment. Confirming its suitability with them and the social worker, I arranged to buy it.

I had heard about a Home Foundation scheme being set up by Mencap whereby the marginally handicapped can live in the community under supervision. With the unpredictable nature of my health, it seemed a suitable way of safeguarding Gina's future and I made enquiries. After viewing the property with Gillian Nicholls from Mencap it was deemed admirable and I donated it to the project. For some reason the Social Service worker did not approve and Gina's four flatmates were surreptitiously moved into an overcrowded council house. Gina moved back in with us pending preparation of the house for Mencap, who welcomed the opportunity of filling the empty places with applicants on their waiting list. The refurbishment now completed, they moved in on 3 February 1984.

In September 1983 I received a letter from Brian Rix, then Secretary General of Mencap expressing their gratitude for the gift of the house, and being the first parent to do so, hoped that it would be an example to others. He reassured me that Gina's future would be in safe and caring hands. This has now been the case for over twenty four years, along with the many others who during that period, have benefited from the accommodation.

For ourselves we bought a modern detached house with double garage in Wood End, a close by cul-de-sac. Built on the former site of Army quarters, once occupied by the late Earl Wavell, when he was commandant of the Aldershot District. I frequently dug up horse shoes in my garden, where once stood the stables.

The proceeds from the sale of the Boundary Road properties were sufficient to cover the cost of our house and the Mencap home. However I later received an unexpected demand for £12,500 Capital Gains Tax on the proceeds of the four flats. As this had been used for the purchase of the house donated to Mencap, a registered charity, I hotly disputed it, even to the extent of visiting my Tax Inspector in Cardiff, but to no avail. Because the money from the flats had passed through my bank account, though only briefly, I had to pay-up.

Mentioning this to our local MP Julian Critchley, on his electioneering rounds, he asked me to send him the details. Eventually I received a letter from the Houses of Parliament signed by John Moore, the Financial Secretary to the Treasury, saying that the tax would be refunded, and which I duly received plus interest.

Travel seems to predominate my diary entries for the next decade or so, both in the UK and abroad, including three memorable cruises. The first was in June 1985 for three weeks in the Mediterranean on the *S.S. Canberra*. In Cyprus we met up with Angie Bath, who as a trainee nurse at the Cambridge, practised bed-bathing me, and was now at the Army hospital in Limassol where we were anchored. Her mother was visiting her and they were ferried aboard joining us for breakfast, before a day sight-seeing ashore in her car.

Then in Haifa we met Barbara and Clive as arranged, who were on holiday there, and after an interesting and enjoyable day in the surrounding area, they came aboard for dinner.

The ship was so much to our liking, easy access to the open deck, good company at our table, which included the ships medical officer, that we had to repeat the experience. This we did in July 1987, on a cruise to Madeira, Portugal and Spain.

The *Canberra* then being out of service, our next cruise was aboard the *QE2* to Norway and Denmark in August 1989. I remember seeing the film 'Amadeus' in the ship's cinema, in which my step cousin Charles Kay played a leading role, a picture of him in the part appearing on the front of the 'Radio Times'.

Six other holidays abroad included three weeks in South Africa in February 1988. We first flew to Johannesburg to visit Vicky's son who had completed his South African Police service, and was then the area representative for 'Famous Grouse' whisky. En route we stopped at Nairobi to refuel, for which I learned there was usually a finagle over the fee. I got out to stretch my legs and followed the disembarking passengers into reception to take a quick look round when suddenly the doors slammed shut behind me. With the Tannoy bawling in Swahili, and with no means of identification, I tried to find a way out, but failed. An official took me into a room where four armed policemen were seated, and told me to wait. Through the window I could see that refuelling was finished, and also Vicky alongside an air hostess, looking very worried. At last the doors opened and I rapidly returned to a relieved Vicky. Back in the aircraft, I wondered if my release was reflected in the rate charged for the fuel.

Passing over the peak of Mount Kilimanjaro, we arrived in Johannesburg 6,000ft above sea level, which took a little while to get acclimatized. We stayed in the Sandton Sun, a twenty storey hotel overlooking a wide expanse of the city. Several outings with Michael and wife Wendy, included a visit to Sun City in Bophuthatswana with its varied attractions.

We had booked to travel on the Blue Train to Cape Town to visit Bab's half-sister Sheila, but owing to the line being flooded in the Orange River area it was cancelled, and we went by air. Sheila and husband John met us where we were staying at the Mount Nelson Hotel. John her second husband had been in the South African Navy, and they met when he was serving in England.

Sarah her daughter from her first marriage who I knew as a child, was now back in England again and had visited us with her son Simon, and later with her second husband Mark who she married during a spell back in South Africa.

Our air-conditioned room overlooked Table Mountain. With the waiters in Raj style costume reminded me of India, and the atmosphere was similar to Raffles Hotel in Singapore. Swimming in the oasis pool and an evening stroll through Government Walk and the Botanical Gardens, was a relief from the sweltering heat.

John arranged to take us to the Simonstown Naval Dockyard, stopping on the way to view the spectacular scenery at False Bay. Similarly staggering was the landscape when returning from lunch one day at the Groot Constantia vineyard via Chapmans Peak, Cape Point and Hout Bay.

We returned to Johannesburg by A300 Air Bus, this time staying at the Balalaika Hotel with its native style thatched roofs. Michael took us on several trips, the first to Pretoria with its memorials and streets lined with Jacaranda trees. On the way we drove through the Krugersdorp game reserve taking close-up snaps of the uncaged lions. In Gold Reef City, after lunch in the Crown restaurant we were entertained with Zulu war dancing, with topless females singing to the rhythm of the drums. At the adjoining gold mine the processing of the raw metal was demonstrated, finally being melted and poured into 12.5 kilogram nuggets.

Before flying back to the UK on 12 March we went shopping in the SandtonCentre and took a final glimpse of the city from the viewing platform on the fiftieth floor of the Carlton Tower. Our flight from Jan Smuts (Johanneburg International) airport was held up due to bad weather and when we eventually boarded the plane at 10pm the visibility was still so bad I could barely see the tail of the aircraft. The pilot was driven down the runway on the fire tender to check the situation, and as the fog gradually lifted we took off at 11pm arriving at Heathrow at 08.45am GMT, the following day.

We continued to take our annual break in the beach bungalow at West Bexington. Further afield we went by coach on a variety of vacations in Scotland, Ireland and Wales. Later, we celebrated Vicky's seventieth birthday on holiday in the Imperial Hotel, Torquay,

We still visited our scattered relatives, Benny and Val having moved to Norwich near their son Simon and wife Sally and family, and Vicky's son now divorced and back in the UK living in Huntingdon. Clocking up a considerable mileage over the years, we changed the Maxi for an Austin Maestro in 1985 and a Peugeot 309 in 1990.

In May 1985 we attended Johnny Palmer's inauguration ceremony in Lewes, as Chairman of the East Sussex Council. Two months later we unexpectedly met him again with his wife Vera and daughter Marion, at a Royal Garden Party, my third, at Buckingham Palace. Sadly we only met once again before he died from a stroke in 1999.

The extension to the Farnborough College was completed in 1987 and officially opened by Sir George Porter, President of the Royal Society, in March 1989. He described its steel and glass structure as a magnificent example of innovative design. It boasts the longest indoor mall in Europe with interior landscaping on a Japanese theme around my former avenue of Cedar trees, and has won several awards. Since then it has been dubbed a design disaster and would have been better built in traditional brick construction.

Now, when walking to the shops, I cut through the college grounds sometimes sitting on a seat on the spot where we once lived. Contemplating how things might have been had we remained there, reminded me of the following final phrase from a poem 'The Water Mill':-

'Take this proverb to thine heart, take and hold it fast,
The Mill cannot grind with the water that is past'. – ANON

My sister Cissie had been in and out of hospital in recent years and on 26 January 1993 was admitted to the Intensive Care Unit at Frimley Park Hospital. We visited her daily along with the other members of the family, including her son Michael from Saudi Arabia who had notified his brother Max in Canada. She was now in a side ward when on 22 February we were urgently called to the hospital. Vicky and I stayed overnight and were with her when she died at 5.30am in the morning, aged 83.

In May that year I woke in the night with pain in my chest and arm, the symptoms of a heart attack and once again I was taken by ambulance to the Cambridge Military Hospital intensive care unit. I lay awake wondering if I was to undergo my experience here in 1983 (Chapter 1). The next day however, I was moved into the main ward and subjected to the rapid routine of the seven-step, one week recovery programme. After this I was discharged on medication and barred from driving for two months.

The Cambridge was closed down in 1996, and medical records stored in Aquilla, a government establishment in Kent. I later learned that these were available to patients on request subject to any item which might cause distress, being withheld. I applied and eventually two 3 inch thick packages arrived and, needless to say there was no record of my heart stoppage in 1983.

Vicky was now undergoing treatment for diabetes, signs of which we first noticed when she developed an unquenchable thirst whilst on holiday in Kitzbühel in 1991. With diet and daily testing her blood sugar level, which had been over twenty, was now down to an acceptable level. She was also experiencing increasingly frequent spells of dizziness and noises in the ear, diagnosed as Ménière's disease and Tinnitus Aurium. However she still performed daily on our Hammond organ and playing by ear, her repertoire was boundless.

Gina had been developing rheumatoid arthritis and with frequent swelling of knees and wrists it had now reached the stage where she would no longer continue in full employment at the hospital, and left after twenty years in the NHS. With acupuncture and medication she remains reasonably active and is always cheerful. As more has become known about Autism I am sure that her personality pattern and retentive memory, fits into its wide spectrum of symptoms, most likely the Aspergers syndrome. At Knellwood where she has accompanied the tea trolley on its Monday morning rounds for sixteen years, she knows the names of the fifty or so residents, and their precise preferences.

During a routine kidney scan in July 1999 it was discovered that I had an aneurysm of the abdominal aorta, a bulge in the main artery which measured 4.4cms instead of the normal 2cms. I was referred to the vascular surgeon who arranged for it to be checked every three months, a major operation being necessary to prevent a fatal rupture, should the swelling increase. There being no adverse effects until it bursts, many have died, including Albert Einstein, and now about 3,000 a year, without it being diagnosed. As a trauma can trigger the condition, I wondered if my heart stoppage experience was the cause.

I put my thinking cap on pondering priorities of preparation for either possibility. My first action in 'clearing the deck' was to dispose of my share portfolio, dealing in which had been a daily task. The Footsie 100 Index then at 4,000 provided a pleasing profit, but with it nearing 7,000 later on, I was somewhat premature.

The quarterly aorta scans were showing a slight increase and by 2001 had reached 4.8cms. That year did not end on a good note. I had parked the car after dropping Vicky off at the nearby shopping centre, and was crossing the road to join her. I was struck by a car which I had not seen and found myself spread out on its bonnet. As the lady driver suddenly braked I was flung into the middle of the road, my face bleeding and my glasses smashed.

Several people came to help and I heard a man shout 'don't move him' as he dialled 999 on his mobile. A young lady, I wish I knew who she was, knelt down and held my hand whilst trying to keep me talking as I drifted in and out of consciousness. The ambulance and police car arrived and as I was being lifted on to a stretcher, I told them that my wife was in Sainsbury's and the police went to find her. Summoned to the check-out by Tannoy she left the trolley and its contents, and came running to the ambulance where they were bandaging my head.

In the A&E at Frimley Park Hospital I was attended to by a senior male army nurse, one of the medical staff transferred from the Cambridge, when it closed. Stripped and examined and no bones broken it was just a case of recovering from the shock and treating the cut's and grazes on my face. Vicky was given lunch and by late afternoon I was back on my feet, and we were able to return home by taxi.

Looking a sorry sight with my face plastered with patches, we called on our neighbour Dr Bill Alston, recently retired from the hospital, and gave him the keys to the car, which he kindly collected for me from the car park.

2003 was the year when things hit rock bottom. It started with the news that Vicky's brother Terry and his wife Joan were both in Bromley Hospital having fallen down the stairs together. Joan never fully recovered and was later re-admitted and died on 17 September.

In June, my sister-in-law Peggy, the Dowager Lady Petre, died aged 87. Her son John, now Lord Lieutenant of Essex, arranged a very private unannounced funeral.

Later that month my sister Eileen was in hospital for an urgent colostomy, but unfortunately died on the 30 June in her ninety-first year. Christopher's son Dominic took me to her funeral service in Maidstone.

My latest aorta scan showed an increase to 5.07cms and I was made aware that with any further increase, the operation was 'on the cards'.

On 12 October Barbara and Clive had just left after their usual Sunday morning visit. Vicky went upstairs whilst I was preparing lunch, and suddenly called out for me. 'I can't feel my head' she said as I entered her bedroom, and she then passed out. I got her on to her bed and called the duty doctor. Being Sunday I thought there maybe some delay so I also rang Bill Alston, next door. I could tell he knew it was something serious, as did the duty doctor who called for an ambulance. As the driver and the paramedic came into the room she briefly regained consciousness and said 'Reg, what are all these men doing here'.

After an initial examination in A&E, the lady doctor knelt down beside my chair to warn me of the precarious nature of her condition, and that she was being taken into the assessment ward. I rang Barbara and Clive who came immediately. Clive stayed by the bedside whilst Barbara ran me home to collect what I would need for the overnight stay in the ward, and to notify her son and brother, and to tell

Gina. A lounger was placed by the bedside for me to put my feet up but I didn't sleep, hoping she might rally. Next morning I went home by taxi to notify the relatives and friends, and await the arrival of Michael and partner Sandy and then return with them to the hospital where Terry and his sister-in-law Judy joined us. She remained unconscious and later we went for a meal together before their departure.

Visiting the following day I was informed that a scan had confirmed a blockage in the right side of the brain. That evening nurse Jennifer rang to say that Vicky had been moved into a single room in the isolation ward where I visited her next morning, the 15 October, and stayed until 4pm. Dominic visited her in the evening and then called in to see me. After he left the ward sister rang to tell me that Vicky had died at 8.10pm. Though not unexpected it was still a grievous shock, and I tried to hold back the tears whilst telephoning everyone concerned. Dominic very kindly came back to see how I was coping.

I lay awake all that night trying to come to terms with my dolorous dilemma, deliberating the daunting tasks that lay ahead for me in my eighty-eighth year.

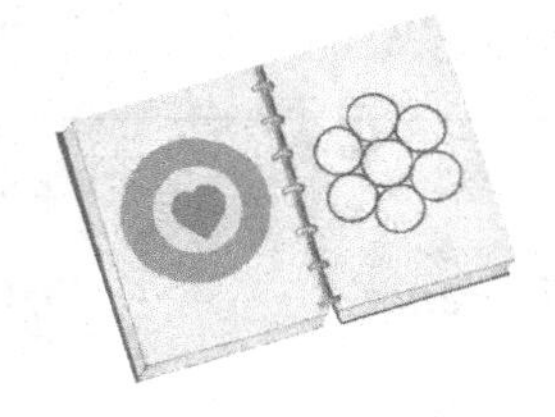

Chapter 6

(2003-2007) 'Into the Sunset'

Making arrangements for the funeral I had to take account of Vicky's disenchantment with the church though still believing in God. Without having knowingly influenced her, it was similar to my own stance since 'seeing the light', and its devinatory effect, that God was directly approachable devoid of the divisive faiths founded by man. Discussing this with the funeral director, a Humanist service was suggested and I was put in touch with Jan Frances of the British Humanist Association.

I stressed to her that Vicky was by no means an atheist, believing in a direct approach to God, without the trappings of religion. She included these very words in her all embracing eulogy, along with the following from a card which Vicky kept by her bedside:-

'God grant me the serenity to accept the things I cannot change,

The courage to change the things I can

And the wisdom to know the difference'

The service at Aldershot Crematorium on 27 October was well attended by relatives and friends. We all stood up to sing 'I Vow to Thee My Country' from Holst's 'Jupiter Suite', Vicky's opening tune when playing the organ, and which contains the immortal words by Cecil Spring Rice:-

'The love that never falters, the love that pays the price,
The love that makes undaunted the final sacrifice'.

The closing of the curtain at the conclusion of the service marked a traumatic juncture in my life. She will live long in the memory of all who knew her, and we gathered together for a remembrance reception at the Queens Hotel.

Her ashes were buried in her brother's Roy's grave in the military section of Brookwood Cemetery. He was killed in a flying accident during the war whilst serving in the Fleet Air Arm, and Vicky, then in the WAAF, had attended the funeral. The grave is in a very tranquil and well-kept setting which I frequently visited whilst I still had the car.

The days flew by with so much to do, including frequent solicitor appointments enacting Vicky's will, and amending mine to fit my new circumstance, and donating my body to medical research. The little known 'deed of variation' whereby the surviving spouse can, within two years, alter their late partner's will, was also applicable. By two such deeds adding to the bequest list in Vicky's will, I was able to help others beyond the otherwise taxable limit.

There were two wardrobes of Vicky's clothes and a colossal collection of shoes, all neatly stored, which I took in several batches to local charity shops.

On the 14 January 2004 a routine ultra scan revealed an increase to 5.4cms. Within two days I received a letter admitting me to the hospital on 20 January for the operation; just three days in which to prepare the house for my absence. This included finding a new home for Sophie the cat who, missing Vicky, was now latching on to me and was good company.

Dominic drove me to the hospital where I was allotted a bed in the military staffed ward F2, where my nurse was a WAAF named Vicky! A CT scan gave a more accurate reading of 5.6cm and I didn't sleep much that night and for some reason, I was prompted to consider cancelling the operation. Next morning the army ward sister invited me into her office to discuss the matter and having made up my mind not to go ahead, she notified the surgical staff. Though they sympathised with my circumstances they pointed out the possible risk of a rupture having refused the operation. I returned home that afternoon with no Sophie to greet me.

At a subsequent appointment with Mr Leopold, the vascular surgeon, I was relieved when he told me that a close examination of the CT scan indicated that it would have been hazardous to operate, the aneurysm being close to the kidney artery.

However, he referred me to Mr Gerard who was investigating an alternative form of operation which might be applicable. This was being performed at a hospital in Liverpool and if I was prepared to go there, Mr Gerard said he would accompany me, to witness the *modus operandi*. The 'guinea pig' aspect did not appeal, and being so far removed from relatives and friends, I did not accept the offer. A three-monthly ultra scan was arranged to assess the situation. Although it was like living with a time bomb ticking away and which was not going to be de-fused, I accepted it with stoical calmness.

Terry having eyesight problems with age-related macular degeneration, was no longer driving and offered to sell me his recently purchased Peugeot 206. My driving licence being valid to March 2007 I readily accepted and went with Christopher and Dominic to collect it, after taking Terry out to lunch.

On Sunday 2 April 2006, Christopher arranged a family gathering at the Bush Hotel in Farnham to celebrate my ninetieth birthday. So many turned up from as far afield as Canada, that we filled the dining room. With a buffet self-service meal it was an ideally informal affair, until a sword was removed from its scabbard and handed to me to cut the cake!

As a birthday card, Christopher's friend Deidre Muir sent me, very appropriately, a copy of Shakespeare's verse about the seven ages of man from 'As You Like It' (see Appendix 1). Although I had only met her once I realised she was a very thoughtful person and I wondered which stage she considered I had reached. Regarding the seventh stage, I would have specified 'Sans hearing' which I find to be the foremost failing feature of that final phase.

I had started writing the early days of these memoirs but realised that more spare time would be needed to complete them, without the chores of housekeeping and gardening. I considered a move into sheltered accommodation but as this would still entail shopping and cooking, and now in my nineties, a retirement home was what I really needed. What more convenient than 'Knellwood' (p.157), just round the corner and near the Mencap home where Gina is resident, and I made inquiries. I booked a short trial period in July, and with my GP being on the committee, I was convinced it met my requirements, and I immediately put the house up for sale.

Although knowing this would be a lengthy procedure, there was still much to be done. The large loft over the double garage in addition to that in the house, were full of items collected over the years, which needed sorting for disposal. Barry Stokes who worked for Hilder when building our house in Boundary Road, was a great help; making countless calls in his car clearing the clutter. The organ which without Vicky had remained silent, I gave to his wife Judy who had befriended Vicky in recent times. I also off-loaded on her, a large amount of kitchen utensils, crockery and cutlery. Items of furniture were sold and family treasures handed over to relatives.

Once the house had been advertised I had twenty viewings in two weeks, and by mid-September was able to accept a satisfactory offer. The buyer having to first sell his own house, meant more time for clearing mine. A local charity was very helpful, collecting such items as spare beds and bedding up to the very end.

It was now three years since Vicky died and on 15 October I went to Brookwood with Gina, Michael and Sandy to pay our respects.

On 4 December I signed a contract taking over the room reserved for me on the first floor of the modern wing of 'Knellwood', overlooking the park-like grounds. I fitted it out with my own items of furniture, particularly my writing bureau, before taking up residence on 12 December 2006.

Though still reasonably active there comes a time in the seasons of ones life when you should live more contemplatively, for every life has a beginning and an end. Which reminds me of the quip:- 'If I would have known I'd live this long, I would have taken better care of myself'.

Completion of the sale of the house was on 15 December, when I handed over the keys. Much to my surprise, the proceeds were paid into my nominated account that very day, the interest on which is sufficient to cover the current charge at my new abode.

Gina came here over Christmas staying in the guest room, and she still comes Monday mornings, helping with the tea trolley. Her knowing the names of all the staff, there being almost as many as there are residents to cover day and night duty, has helped me getting to know them individually. Their dedication and commitment is remarkable, and I hope they are rewarded with a feeling of self-satisfaction for helping others.

The day to day management under the matron and the staff being predominately female, accounts for the overall efficiency and effectiveness in the running of the Home. I'm sure the Chairman and bursar and other male members of the committee and staff will understand what I mean.

I won't pursue this seemingly gender preference except to say that I thought it to be wrong when the Womens Armed

Services were disbanded to enlist them alongside their male counterparts, on an equal footing. With different aptitudes in many respects women are 'more than equal', such as superior exam results, especially when in single-sex schools, not to mention womanhood bearing the birth of mankind. I could have written an article on the subject under some such title as 'The Hand That Rocks the Cradle Rules the World'.

Quoting from the 'Knellwood' handbook: 'The home exists primarily for active, able-bodied people who might be expected to enjoy all the amenities of a comfortable country house for years on end, and the staffing and catering are conducted on these lines'. Comes the time of course with creeping decrepitude, a proportion of residents need tending by the caring staff. Then eventually, they would normally be replaced with more active applicants.

Unfortunately, despite a shortage of housing, the government encourages the elderly to remain in their homes, with ever decreasing and more expensive home-help, and the majority of those aged over 75, live alone. Consequently, new residents arrive at a stage, some in wheelchairs, when they can no longer fend for themselves, creating a disproportionate burden on the caring staff.

With ever increasing longevity, there is a growing need for more non-profit making, charity registered homes similar to 'Knellwood', each supported by a local fund raising body comparable to the Companions of Knellwood to which I have contributed for many years. Apart from covering the cost of new items of furniture and fittings, they provide presents and excursions for the residents. On 17 April 2007, I was one of a small group taken to see 'The Phantom of the Opera' at Her Majesty's Theatre, after lunching in the West End.

On the expiry of my driving licence on my ninety-first birthday, I sold the Peugeot 206, the last of the fourteen different cars which I had owned over the years. Now my frequent visits to the shops entail slowly walking the one and a half miles each way combating claudication, the pain in my calves due to poor circulation. My occasional need for a taxi is well within the cost of running a car.

At a routine scan on 26 July, the aneurysm which had remained a steady 5.7cms for several months had shot up to 6.0cms. I thought of plotting a graph of its growth over the eight years of scanning to trace a trend, but didn't dare as it seemed like trying to determine the date of my demise. I was asked if, in the event of it bursting, and I was taken to the hospital in time, did I want them to try a repair, to which, not knowing when this book would be finished, I replied 'Yes'.

'Enjoying all the amenities of a country house' has enabled me to so far bring these memoirs up-to-date. Not having any computing ability, I have written them in long hand, sending them in batches to my step-niece Sarah, who produces the draft typescript on her lap-top with amazing speed, for my approval. She then provides several copies for eventual perusal by potential publishers, when it is completed.

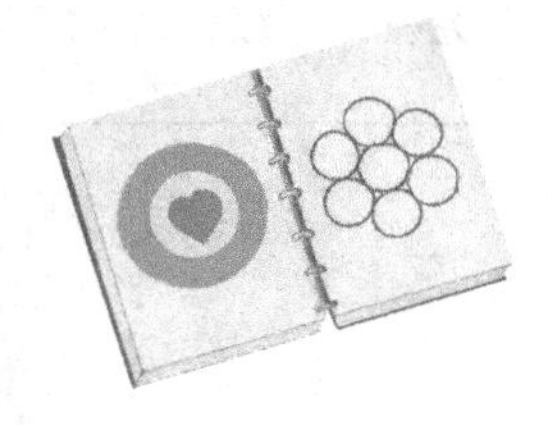

Chapter 7

'A New Dawn'

Each of us from midwife's slap
Know not how long till our final nap,
Whether the span be long or short
All should record what life has taught.

Since my thirty seven years service in the RAF, I have been another thirty seven years in retirement. For how long this will be extended 'God alone knows' (my mother's favourite remark). Hopefully long enough to put the last piece of the jigsaw in place by finishing this final chapter, through chinks of which I pray that rays of 'the light' will beam.

i ***Heart and Head***

I must first refer to two different parts of our mental life, one which 'feels' and the other which 'thinks'; the emotional and the rational, interacting with each other to determine our outlook.

The range of our emotions, excitement, fear, anger, good or evil, must be directed to form an intuitive moral code of honesty, integrity, and to discern the difference between right and wrong. This is the basis of Pelmanism, right feeling and right thinking create right willing (action).

Feeling, the motivation which directs the mind, needs the numinous nourishment of prayer, just as the body needs a balanced diet. Prayer is devoting the heart and mind to God. 'More things are wrought by prayer than this world dreams of' (Tennyson).

Prince Philip reflecting on the big questions of life in his book 'Down to Earth' observes that man's relationship to the natural world is not a matter of science, it is a matter of 'concept and conscience'.

ii Science

Science is about what can be proved or disproved, it teaches us nothing about values, ethics or morals. Though the theory of evolution rightly refutes the seven day creationism in the bible, science does not undermine the concept of God. Some neuro-scientist's now believe that there is a genetic propensity for us to personally know God, that we are programmed with an intuition of the divine as a distinguishing disposition of mankind.

This spiritual gene, the 'inner-voice' is more developed in some than others, but most accept an infinite God as the supreme creator of the fundamental laws of science, the only universal language.

Science continues to unwrap the magnificence of the universe. 'Mystery is the fundamental emotion which stands in the cradle of true science' (Albert Einstein).

iii Atheism

The atheistic denial of the existence or concept of God ranges from the dogmatic to the speculative. The latter would apply to Humanists who whilst believing in helping others, remain impervious to the 'inner-voice' which is prompting them. The former who unequivocally deny God claim that the universal laws and evolution came about by blind chance and/or natural selection.

However it is worth noting the experience of one of the most militant atheists, the famous philosopher, the late Sir Alfred Ayer (1910-1989). In 1988 he was in the University College Hospital suffering from pneumonia when he had a near death experience, his heart having stopped for four minutes. Later he wrote 'I was confronted by an exceedingly bright light which I became aware was responsible for the government of the universe and it altered my adamant attitude that there is no life after death'.

Whilst still in intensive care Dr George, the duty doctor who had been at New College, Oxford when Ayer was there as Professor of Logic, asked him as a philosopher, what it was like to have a N.D.E. He replied 'I saw a divine being; I'm afraid I'll have to revise all my various books and opinions. This he never did as he died the following year, but the experience had noticeably enhanced his approach to life and to his associates.

Perhaps if Richard Dawkins had a similar experience he would revise his book 'The God Delusion' in which the only reference to the post death experience, is when he includes it in a list of what he refers to as 'hilarious arguments for the existence of God'. Yet when discussing the probability of God he leaves the door slightly ajar, giving an assessment of 6 in a spectrum of 1 to 7.

'SANS DIEU RIEN' is a sign displayed on the clock tower over the forecourt entrance at Ingatestone Hall – 'without God there is nothing'.

iv The Post Death Experience

Professor Ayer's experience correlates to the core pattern of that encountered by the numerous cases which have been investigated over recent decades, documented in many books. Typical of these is 'The Truth in the Light' by Dr Peter Fenwick, consultant neuro-psychiatrist and President of the International Association of Near Death Studies. I wrote to him in 1994 with an account of my experience, which helped in his research. I was referred to a TV Production Company who were making a programme on the subject for Channel 4, but I declined the offer to participate.

Most accounts feature the following:- separation from the body, entering into darkness then seeing the 'light', crossing over into its peace and tranquillity and meeting former figures who had featured in their life. Then back in the body, the incommunicable nature of the event, and its enrichment of perception and perspective.

Prior to my own encounter, the thought of donating a property to Mencap, or boosting the bequests in Vicky's will, would not have entered my head. Maybe the event somehow increases the discharge of the hormone oxytocin from the pituary gland, proved to promote a philanthropic persuasion.

Apart from these more recent occurrences of N.D.E.'s, the countless number over time immemorial, in all parts of the world, proclaiming life after death, have been the soteriological basis of the redemption of mankind, for which many different doctrines have been devised.

v ***Religion***

Louis Pasteur (1822-99) wrote 'So long as the mystery of God weighs on the human mind, so long will temples be raised by different cults whether they be called Brahma, Allah, Jehovah or Jesus'.

In his recent book 'The Story of God' the well-known scientist Lord Robert Winston, researches the roots and rites of religions world-wide, representing different paths to an Almighty God. Discussing the disparities within each faith he mentions the little known sects of Judaism, the 'Christian Jews' and another not believing in an after life.

When religion is identified with state power, it has often caused conflict and carnage throughout history, between rival countries and cults, and between sects within a particular religion. This accounted for the Crusades in the eleventh and twelfth centuries, the holocaust of the Jews in Germany, the blood baths involved in the partitioning of Ireland and more recently that of India.

The present problem is the threat of widespread terrorism by those who are indoctrinated to believe that to forego their own life in destroying the infidel, is a way to their salvation.

Tony Blair is finalising plans to set-up an international faith foundation to ease the tension between the world's major religions and to tackle misunderstanding, particularly with Islam. Presumably he is not unaware of Tolerance International, already well established to deal with this very problem, helping those suffering the effects of religious fanaticism and the oppression of women.

Regarding the different denominations of Christianity there are various views on the divinity of Jesus Christ. The undogmatic Unitarians reckon that he was a man, no more or less than a man, who revealed the power, the wisdom and love of God, and that his preaching was about a way of life related to God and ones fellow beings.

The non-conformist Quakers, founded by George Fox in the seventeenth century is also based on the teaching of Christ, and that God is readily accessible to all without any defined creed or channel of communication. This and their practice of unprogrammed silent worship is commendable, but like other denominations there are diversities of detail, a substantial number still conceding a uniquely divine character to Christ.

The incarnate concept of God in human form is misleading and unnecessary. If it were to have been so, surely it should have featured a female figure rather than a male, the 'Mother of Mankind' making a much more motivational immortal image! Incidentally in the Church of England there are now more female than male clergy being ordained.

Without delving into the realm of academic theology, I would like to mention that in which part of the world you were born, East or West, can determine which if any is your religious belief, or even if it was in the North or South of Ireland. Had the Pope been born in Tibet, he could be the Dalai Lama, or if in England, the protestant Archbishop of Canterbury.

Branding with baptism and the like, soon after birth, followed by brain washing at an impressionable age, and with repetitive practices such as the rosary, usually determines ones belief for life.

I agree with Richard Dawkins' statement in 'The God Delusion' – 'There is no such thing as a Christian child, only a child of Christian parents'; which of course also applies to other faiths.

Children should be taught a strict moral code of good behaviour and social responsibility in secular schools, their minds being left wide open until they become aware of the 'inner-light'. Then they will have no need for faith or belief for they will know God, validated by their open-hearted feelings and thoughts being enthused and directed on a path of righteousness and good works. With these you can awaken the awareness in others, but you can only prove God to yourself.

The Greeks better understood the mysterious power of the hidden side of things. They bequeathed to us one of the most meaningful words in our language 'Enthusiasm' – (*en theos*) – 'God within'.

vi Scepticism

I use the term scepticism to cover all, including agnostics, who are in the 'no-mans land' of doubt regarding God. Tennyson in his poem 'In Memoriam' states 'there lies more faith in honest doubt, believe me, than in half the creeds'. Some however are oblivious to God being too pre-occupied with the cares of daily existence.

A large number, judging from the rapid decline in church attendance, have either decided to escape from being trapped in the religion of their upbringing doubting its authenticity, or have just drifted into materialism. Many lapsed Catholics have become disillusioned with changes in the codes of practice since the 1960's, the Tridentine Latin Mass being replaced by a vernacular version, and now recently restored by Pope Benedict XVI.

There has always been changes, in early times the rood screen separated the congregation from the sanctity and mystery of the Mass. In time this partition took the form of a symbolic wrought iron frame. I remember in our church at Brook Green when the metal uprights of this screen at the high altar were removed to give more room for communicants at the altar rail below, waiting for the priest to place a host on their tongue. Now this can be done by a lay member of either sex, and with declining attendance at Mass, the extra space is no longer needed. The layout of the altar has been re-arranged so that the priest now faces his fading flock.

Former convent buildings in Farnborough are now used as office blocks, and the local Salesian College, previously staffed from the Salesian fraternity, now has a lay headmaster.

When I first came here in the 1950's, St Michaels Abbey was a hive of activity attracting a large congregation for Mass on Sundays. Then there were a dozen or more monks busily occupied in their spare time, wood-carving, book-binding and weaving clerical vestments with silk from their farm of silkworms. Some of this was used in the making of the coronation robes for our Queen, Elizabeth II.

Now with minimal manning of the monastery such activities have ceased, and like many churches with a scarcity of clergy, for most of the time the entrance gates remain closed. Fortunately the gateway to God is always open.

Starting with the more rational regions of civilisation, man-made religion will eventually vanish into the archives of history.

To those in doubt and are discarding their religion I say don't become an atheist and throw the 'baby' out with the bathwater, but develop an awareness of the 'inner-light', the true intrinsic knowledge of God.

When to the flowers beautiful
The good God gave their name,
Back came a little blue-eyed one
So timidly it came.
'Dear God the name you gave me
Indeed I have forgot.'
Kindly God smiled and said
'Forget-me-not'.

(Extract from my mother's autograph album c.1908)

vii Juxta Est Alea - (The Die is Cast)

Recently my thought's repeatedly return to my experience in Chapter 1, my minds-eye focussing on when I was surrounded and interconnected with six 'soulmates'. This for some reason, I equate with a pattern of six similar size circles surrounding a seventh, all in contact with each other:-

This is evident when forming
the pattern with seven round
coins of the same value.

Sir Martin Rees the Astronomer Royal in his visionary book 'Just Six Numbers' refers to the deep forces that shape the universe. Six equations, all interconnected, which underpin and play a distinctive role in the laws related to outer space down to the atom.

Reflecting on their common origin and fine-tuning, he mentions the possible providence of a benign creator for this recipe of the universe. This would conveniently be No. 7 in the centre of his six numbers using the above pattern of septenary circles.

I have now conceived the significance of my obsessive attachment to this heptad pattern which has materialized as follows. The concept is to form support groups of seven associates who are, or prepared to be, committed to some form of care in the community.

The plan provides for a widespread fulfilment of the 'Golden Rule', a single theme enshrined in the scriptures of seven of the world's leading religions, the greatest of all virtues – 'Charity'. There are several forms of this, but here we are less concerned with the money raising aspect than in giving time and attention to helping those in need, as in the following also from my mother's autograph album -

I shall pass through this world but once,
Any good thing therefore that I can do
Or any kindness that I can show to any human being,
Let me do it now and not defer it, for I shall not pass this way again

(E. Isted 30 June 1909)

Also in the words of the philanthropist Leonard Cheshire -

'In my opinion, the great mission of those who suffer and are in want,
Is to draw out the inherent goodwill that is in all of us,
And so to make us forget ourselves and draw close
To one another in our common journey through life'.

Any number of groups can be started each by one individual in the centre recruiting six others to complete the pattern and form what I call a 'chapter', its US usage meaning a fraternity. Being the most important part of this book I am using it as the title, 'Chapter Seven'.

There is no formal linkage between chapters; no set rules, no exclusivism of either sex, no headquarters or hierarchy. At an initial get-together in a chapter house, which can be anywhere convenient, the fellowship, each inspired by their inner-light, will decide how they intend to help in the locality. Either collectively or individually, it could be in support of organized charities, care homes, hospices, prisons etc, or focussing on solitary cases of hardship and neglect.

Subsequently, congenial gatherings should be arranged, as required, to report progress and plan ahead, highlighting where help is most needed. No formal agenda, minutes or accounts are needed. Between meetings members will keep in touch with each other as necessary.

The social reformer Arnold Toynbee (1825-83) believed that only those could help the poor who lived among them. Not necessarily so today, but in my situation, living among the aged occupants in *Knellwood*, I can see what he meant. So many instances crop up throughout the day when you can unobtrusively help others, without treading on the toes of the busy caring staff when they are otherwise occupied.

Talking of carers, among the best are those who can smile, a gift which benefits others. Also throughout life I have found that giving praise and encouragement to the young and adolescent, as well as the aged, is effective and rewarding.

'Man is here for the sake of others – above all for those upon whose well being our own happiness depends' (Albert Einstein). You reap what you sow.

In due course, one by one, at different stages each member of a fraternity, other than the leader, will when so motivated, move on to set up their own Chapter 7 after arranging an acceptable replacement in their present group. This form of chain reaction could have a far reaching effect, becoming widespread like the expanding ripples on a pond.

The date is 8 November 2007 and I have just returned from yet another ultra-scan of the abdominal aorta at the former Cambridge Military Hospital, a section of which is being used for outpatients to relieve the traffic congestion at Frimley Park Hospital.

After the scan I was shown to a consulting room, the very same one where Col. Cormack told me that my heart stoppage 24 years ago, nearly made the Guinness Book of Records. I was seen by the vascular consultant nurse specialist Claire Martin (nee King) B.Sc. who has dealt with my progressively increasing aneurysm so understandingly, over the past 8 years. She informed me that it had now reached 6.2cms.

In spite of her kind assuagement stressing the marginality of the recent increase, I know that the time has now come for me to conclude these memoirs if I am to see them in print, whilst the autumn leaves of my life are still falling.

The End

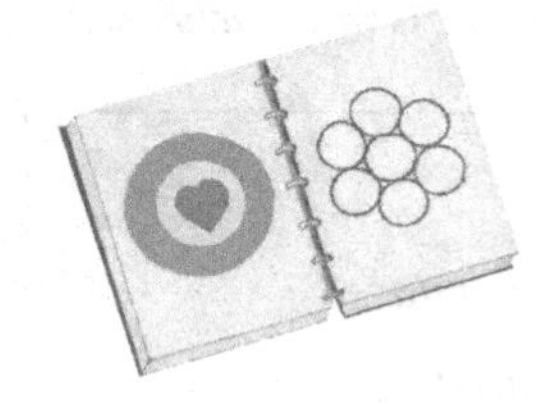

Appendix I

ACT II SCENE VII AS YOU LIKE IT

All the World's a stage,
And all the men and women merely Players:
They have their exits and their entrances;
And one man in his time plays many parts,
His acts being seven ages. At first the infant,
Mewling and puking in the nurses arms.

And then the whining school-boy, with his
satchel, and shining morning face, creeping
like a snail unwillingly to school.

And then the lover, sighing like a furnace,
with a woful ballad made to his mistress'
eyebrow.

Then a soldier, full of strange oaths, and
bearded like the pard, jealous in honour,
sudden and quick in quarrel, seeking the
bubble reputation even in the cannon's
mouth.

And then the justice, in fair round belly with
good cap lin'd,
With eyes severe, and beard of formal cut,
Full of wise saws and modern instances;
And so he plays his part.

The sixth age shifts into the lean and
slipper'd pantaloon, with spectacles on nose
and pouch on side, his youthful hose well
sav'd, a world too wide for his shrunk shank;
And his big manly voice, turning again
toward childish treble, pipes and whistles in
his sound.

Last scene of all, that ends this strange
eventful history, is second childishness and
mere oblivion,
sans teeth, sans eyes, sans taste, sans
everything!

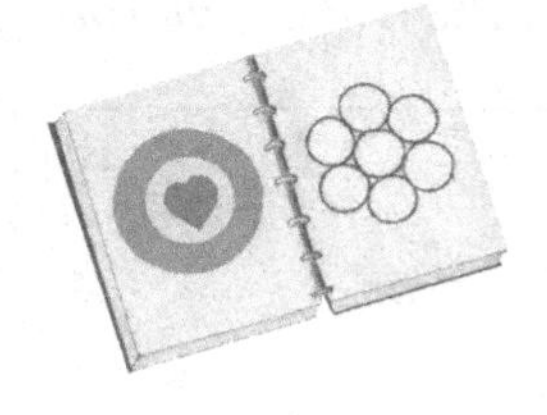

Appendix 2

HONEST TO GOD

The truth oft seems not black and white
But many shades of grey,
Like twilight 'twixt the day and night
When neither one holds sway.

So in fruitless confrontations
When each their own views flout,
Grant, to retain good relations,
Benefit of the doubt.

Yet sometimes though the truth is clear
We still maybe disposed,
Lest it might hurt someone held dear,
To keep the lips well closed.

And with truth be economic
If strife it would entail,
Fingers crossed and be laconic
Let peace and calm prevail.

In this our conscience plays a part,
With judgement from on High,
Pray God forgive a caring heart,
The altruistic lie.

R. Piff

The Voice of Reason (collected Poems)
ISBN: 1-84436-079-2
United Press Ltd. 2004

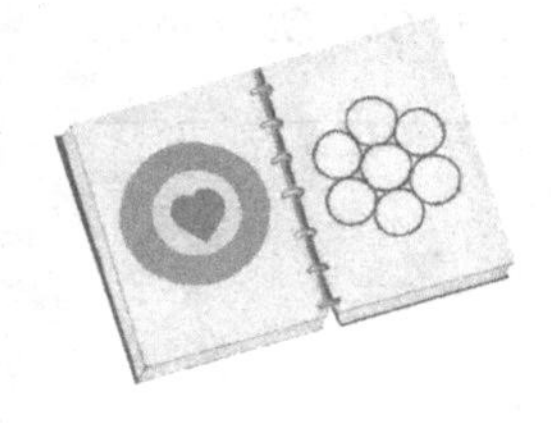

Appendix 3

'Let's Face It' by Christine Piff
ISBN: 0-575-03533-1
Pub: Victor Gollanz Ltd. 1985

'Down to Earth' by Prince Philip
ISBN: 0002190478
Pub: Collins 1988

'The God Delusion' by Richard Dawkins
ISBN: 9780552273317
Pub: Black Swan 2006

'The Truth in the Light' by Peter Fenwick
ISBN: 9780742246688
Pub: Headline 1996

'The Story of God' by Robert Winston
ISBN: 0-593-05493-8
Pub: Bantam Press 2005

'Just Six Numbers' by Sir Martin Rees
ISBN: 9780297842972
Pub: Weidenfeld & Nicholson 1999

'The Voice of Reason' (Collected Poems)
ISBN: 1-844-36079-2
Pub: United Press Ltd. 2004